I0797297

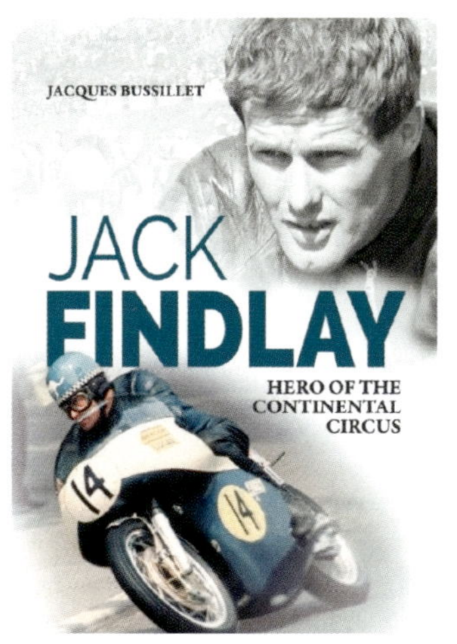
JACQUES BUSSILLET
JACK
FINDLAY
HERO OF THE
CONTINENTAL
CIRCUS
14
14

More great motorcycle books from Veloce

Bimota Story, The (Falloon)
British 250cc Racing Motorcycles (Pereira)
BSA Motorcycles – the final evolution (Jones)
Chris Carter at Large – Stories from a lifetime in motorcycle racing (Carter & Skelton)
Edward Turner – The Man Behind the Motorcycles (Clew)
Fine Art of the Motorcycle Engine, The (Peirce)
Franklin's Indians (Sucher/Pickering/Diamond/Havelin)
India - The Shimmering Dream (Reisch/Falls (translator))
Jim Redman – Six Times World Motorcycle Champion: The Autobiography (Redman)
Kawasaki W, H1 & Z – The Big Air-cooled Machines (Long)
Kawasaki Z1 Story, The (Sheehan)
Mike the Bike – Again (Macauley)
Motorcycles, Mates and Memories (Snelling)
Motorcycle Apprentice (Cakebread)
Motorcycle GP Racing in the 1960s (Pereira)
Motorcycle Racing with the Continental Circus 1920-1970 (Pereira)
Motorcycle Road & Racing Chassis Designs (Noakes)
Motorcycling in the '50s (Clew)
MV Agusta since 1945 (Falloon)
Off-Road Giants! (Volumes 1, 2 and 3) – Heroes of 1960s Motorcycle Sport (Westlake)
Racing Classic Motorcycles (Reynolds)
Racing Line – British motorcycle racing in the golden age of the big single (Guntrip)
Scooter Mania! – Recollections of the Isle of Man International Scooter Rally (Jackson)
'Sox' – Gary Hocking – the forgotten World Motorcycle Champion (Hughes)
Slow Burn – The growth of Superbikes & Superbike racing 1970 to 1988 (Guntrip)
Triumph Motorcycles & the Meriden Factory (Hancox)
TT Talking – The TT's most exciting era (Lambert)
Velocette Motorcycles – MSS to Thruxton (Burris)
Velocette: The Three Twins: Roarer, Model O and LE (Agnew & Rhodes)

Also available as ebooks
See our website for all the latest titles

www.veloce.co.uk

Translated from the French by Alan Cathcart

First published in 2025 by Veloce, an imprint of David and Charles Limited. Tel +44 (0)1305 260068 / e-mail info@veloce.co.uk / web www.veloce.co.uk.
ISBN: 9781836440475 Readers with ideas for automotive books, or books on other transport or related hobby subjects, are invited to write to the editorial director of Veloce at the above address. British Library Cataloguing in Publication Data – A catalogue record for this book is available from the British Library. Design and production by Veloce. Printed and bound in Turkey by Pelikan Printing.

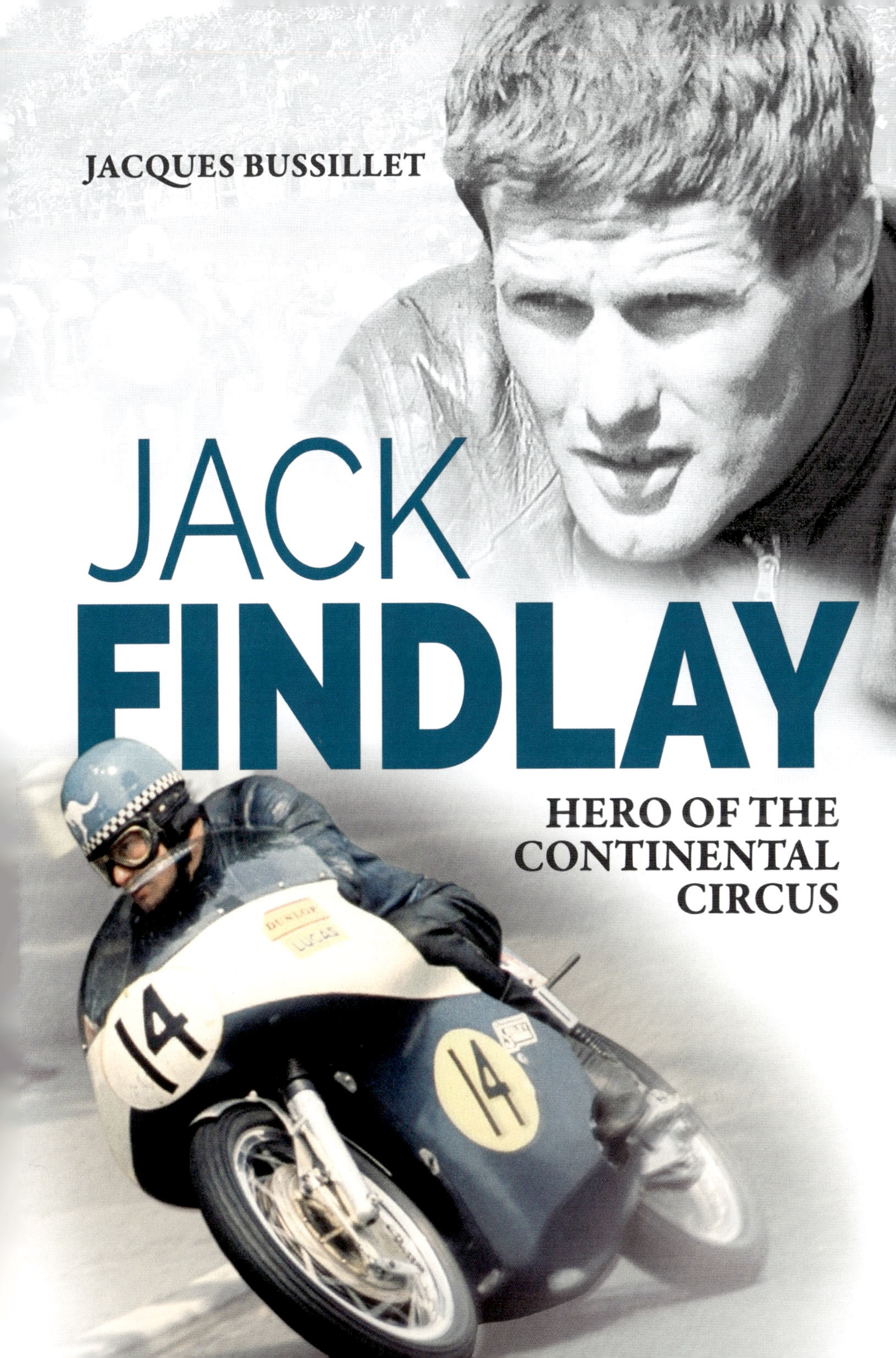
JACQUES BUSSILLET
JACK
FINDLAY
HERO OF THE
CONTINENTAL
CIRCUS

24
4
40

Contents

Foreword

Ya motorcycle racer
Greatest private rider in the world
Lucky time chaser
Greatest private rider in the world
I'm gonna be the fastest rider
Comin' up behind you

Can't you see me Agostini?
Comin' up behind you
Don't you see me Agostini?...
Have to catch ya later, oh yeah

Time is your life
Time is your wife
Time is your world
Just you and your bike
And you're all alone

Foreword

It's hard not to have these verses from *Blues for Findlay* in your head when you think of Jack Findlay, the hero of the movie *Continental Circus*. The song *Blues for Findlay* is the music of Daevid Allen, a musician from the '60s and '70s whose discography reflects those whirlwind years of sex, drugs, rock'n'roll ... and speed.

As luck would have it, I spent two days with Daevid Allen and his musicians in December 1971. Their newly-formed band Gong was on tour to support its newly-released album *Camembert Electrique*. A concert was planned in Strasbourg where I was finishing my studies at the École de Journalisme, while writing my first articles for motorbike magazines. Some friends involved in organising the concert had asked me, because I spoke better English that them, to help them welcome Daevid Allen and his band.

One evening, as we were chatting away, Daevid told me that he was looking forward to the release of a film for which he had composed the music. "Something crazy, about motorbike racing, with guys killing themselves at every bend. I didn't even wait until the end of the first screening to get some riffs in my head and the lyrics just came to me."

I suddenly realised that he was talking about Jérôme Laperrousaz's film, shot in 1969 on the Grand Prix circuits. I told him that I had attended most of the filming that summer, and he confirmed that the hero of the film was indeed Jack Findlay, a compatriot, a neighbour even, since Daevid Allen was born in Melbourne two years after the hero of the film.

By this time I was getting to know Jack and his partner Nanou very well, and I was able to satisfy the curiosity of the musicians who wanted to know more about these nomads who criss-crossed Europe every summer, and whose lives they knew only from the film for which they had produced the music.

Time passed, but my ties with Jack and Nanou, with whom I rubbed shoulders on the circuits between 1970 and 1978, had never broken. In the autumn of 2023, I was contacted by a group of Australian fans who asked me if I would write a book about Jack Findlay. They wanted his story to be preserved, to complement the monument that was erected to his memory in his home town of Mooroopna in 2006.

I wondered why Australians would ask this of me, a Frenchman a long way from them. Before giving my answer, I started looking for documents, photos, articles and interviews from the time. With what I had kept and what I was able to find after contacting a few photographer friends, I was spoilt for choice.

The result is in your hands, for this is the story of this iron man, this incredible motorcycle rider who will for ever be the hero and symbol of the Continental Circus, not forgetting Nanou, his partner in this great adventure.

CHAPTER 1

A Guy Called Jack

Australia, 1950-1957

Cyril John Findlay (called John as a child, but later known as Jack) was born on 5 February, 1935, in Mooroopna, a small Australian town in the state of Victoria, about 200km north of Melbourne. Jack liked to say. "Mooroopna means 'deep waters' in the Aboriginal language, and I've been drowning all my life,' adding, "My ancestors came to Australia to join the gold rush. Maybe that's why I've got adventure in my blood."

Jack's father, also called Jack, of Scottish ancestry, was a bread delivery man, and his mother was called Hazel. He had a younger brother, Robert, and a younger sister, Joan. His father's brother, who owned a motorcycle, took him for rides around race tracks when he was young. Perhaps that's where his passion for racing was born. His brother also recounts that when Jack arrived in Melbourne for work, he came across a man named Butts Pavey, who sped around the city, enjoying being chased by the police without ever being caught. Later, Jack also confided that at around the age of ten, he was fascinated by a photo of bike racer Harry Hinton. It's probably a mixture of all these childhood memories that pushed him to try his luck at racing bikes.

At the age of 14, Jack left school to work at the Commonwealth Bank of Australia as an apprentice accountant. With his first savings and a small loan, he bought a 350 AJS on which he rode alone at night around Melbourne, then signed up for his first race. It was at the end of 1950. Jack was only 15 years old, but the minimum age required to race was 16.

"As soon as it was fully paid off – and it took sacrifices because it cost me four fifths of my meagre salary – I wanted to race with it. It was easy; there were club races everywhere. I started racing in Motocross with that old 350 AJS by lying about my age. Then I had the idea to use my father's name and show his identity card. His name was Jack, so I kept that name forever."

An ardent Aussie rules footballer, Jack trained diligently with the Vermont club, which helped him improve his physical condition. He later confessed that he was good at this sport, and wanted to take up an offer to join the Melbourne Devils AFL team, but he needed to be able to train on Saturday mornings, and his bank manager boss refused to give him this time off. "That's why I gave up football and chose motorbikes."

Jack's deepest passion was indeed motorcycles. For two years he took part in Aussie Short Track races, halfway between Speedway and Motocross, helped by friends from the Nunawading Motorcycle Club. Many of them were faster than him, but they all encouraged him to keep going. One of them,

The birth of a vocation: little John Findlay on his uncle's Levis motorcycle.

John Findlay, the future Jack, is clearly recognisable by his smile in this photo taken at Mooroopna School in 1942.

named John Board, taught him his first basic mechanics. "He was twice as fast as me, but I got better," Jack later admitted.

In the book written by Don Cox dedicated to Australian riders, John Board recounts that he nicknamed Jack Findlay 'Tiger'. "I knew Butts Pavey, and I met Findlay at the club. He had a sluggish motorcycle but an impressive will to race. He worked in the accounting department of a bank, then he went to work as an assistant

Jack poses with his first motorbike, stripped of the accessories he didn't need to race Motocross.

accountant at Watson Victor, a company that made medical equipment."

At the start of 1957, after an injury, John Board suggested that Findlay buy his bike, a Norton special comprising a 1948 long-stroke engine somehow fitted into a much later Featherbed frame. "It was a bike with which I had nothing but problems," said Jack. "The handling was terrible. I think I fell off on every track I took it to. The weight distribution was bad, with the engine too far back, and not enough weight on the front. To top it off, it had a very homemade full aluminium fairing. Fortunately, later that year I was able to buy a 350 Manx Norton, which allowed me

With this Norton Inter, things were about to get serious in real road racing.

Jack on his Norton bitza during a race at Bathurst in 1957.

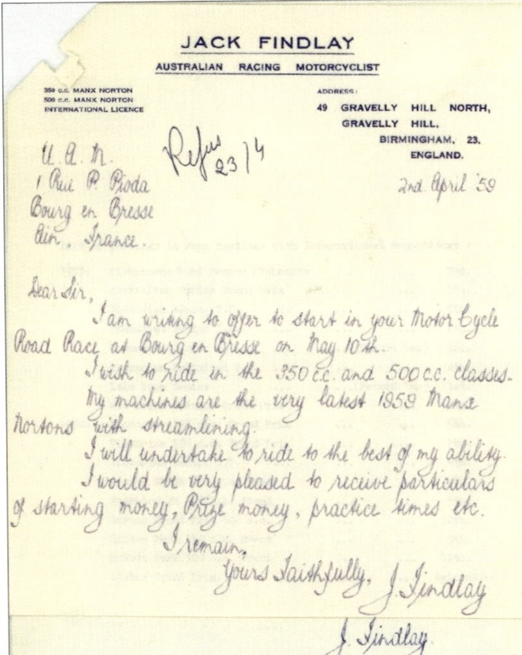

JACK FINDLAY

AUSTRALIAN RACING MOTORCYCLIST

350 c.c. MANX NORTON
500 c.c. MANX NORTON
INTERNATIONAL LICENCE

ADDRESS:
49 GRAVELLY HILL NORTH,
GRAVELLY HILL,
BIRMINGHAM, 23.
ENGLAND.

Refus 23/4

U. A. M.
1 Rue P. Pioda
Bourg en Bresse
Ain, France.

2nd April '59

Dear Sir,

I am writing to offer to start in your Motor Cycle Road Race at Bourg en Bresse on May 10th.

I wish to ride in the 350 c.c. and 500 c.c. classes. My machines are the very latest 1959 Manx Nortons with streamlining.

I will undertake to ride to the best of my ability.

I would be very pleased to receive particulars of starting money, Prize money, practice times etc.

I remain,
Yours faithfully, J. Findlay

J. Findlay

One of Jack's first entry requests in 1959: a handwritten letter, no results list, so a refusal.

Jack on his Norton at the 1959 IOM Tourist Trophy.

The 350cc AJS 7R was the machine used by most privateers in this category.

to improve a bit, both in terms of riding and mechanics." With the humour that always characterised him, he also told Don Cox that his level of riding was "rather horizontal."

Jack married Eileen Kneebone at the end of 1957, and for their honeymoon, he proposed that she should accompany him to England, where he was determined to try his luck on the local race circuits. He had no track record and did not figure among the top Australian riders. Moreover, his friends tried to dissuade him, but a brave heart never stops trying. Jack was driven by an inflexible will – nothing stopped him when he decided to do something.

So in February 1958, a month after finishing fifth in a Victoria TT race in

The famous Manx Norton was the most popular bike in the 500cc class.

Ballarat, he left for England aboard the SS Oronsay, with £30 in his pocket and only his 1956 Manx 350 as capital. Among the passengers was another novice racer, Tom Phillis, with his young wife, Betty. There was also a reigning world champion, Keith Campbell, with his wife Geraldine, and another couple, Harry and Faye Hinton. Via the Suez Canal, the journey took more than two weeks, giving them all time to get to know each other and bond.

Upon arriving in England, harsh reality hit: they each had to find a job to survive. The young couple settled in Birmingham, where Jack found work at the BSA factory. At that time, people in England were hired and paid weekly, making the workforce very mobile. During 1958, Jack would also work for Dunlop, and in a factory subcontracted to weld Morris Mini Minor chassis. Forgetting his assistant accountant training, he got his hands dirty, working like any other labourer.

And, of course, he tried to get involved in some races, but there was no shortage of applicants, and the competition was tough. Jack took a particular hit to his morale when he first set foot on an English circuit. The standard was very high, with everyone really fast, and the quickest ones – those who tried to overtake at each corner – nicknamed 'scratchers'.

It's difficult to keep track of the number of races in which Jack took part during this first season in England, and his attempts to get involved on the Continent. Having only one machine, a 350, he boldly asked for entries in both 350 and 500cc races, taking advantage of the fact that only a trained eye could differentiate between each version of the famous Manx Norton. Records show his entries at Aintree, Brands Hatch and in the Isle of Man Tourist Trophy, where he got a start in the Junior (350) and Senior (500) TT races, but was forced to retire in both.

He also sought to get involved in racing on the other side of the Channel. The best chance for novice riders of the time, the real unknowns, was to get a start at the longer circuits, as the track configuration allowed for a large number of competitors, at least 40, sometimes more. The exception was the TT, a 60.7km (37.7 miles) course where, in good years, there were up to 100 starters in the Junior or Senior races, with the riders released two-by-two every ten seconds.

That summer, Jack secured two entries in Germany. At the Nürburgring in July, he started two races with the same motorcycle. After qualifying well in both categories, he retired after a few laps in the 350 race for fear of a breakdown, as he'd noticed after practice that a gear in the cam drive had a tooth missing, but he had nothing to repair it with. The early stop was necessary because, as the 500 category was the most prestigious, he wanted to be sure of starting that race, and especially to have time to 'convert' his 350 into a 500.

That was one of the basic tricks of the trade in the so-called Continental Circus at that time. The organisers didn't pay particularly close attention during the pre-race technical scrutineering. There was minimal external differentiation between two machines as similar to one another as the 350 and 500 Manx Nortons so, if necessary, you could start the 500 race with a 350. This subterfuge was necessary to collect start money in each category. That was conventional practice for beginner riders, as Jack was that year, or for anyone who hadn't had time to repair a major breakdown. The main thing was to make the trip profitable, for the start money covering travel expenses was meagre and the circuits were scattered all over Europe.

"Fortunately, later that year I was able to buy a 350 Manx Norton, which allowed me to improve a bit, both in terms of riding and mechanics."

At the Nürburgring, the end result was positive, as Jack finished the 500 race in 14th place. It was a good result on this 22km (13.7 miles) circuit, where you must know every turn to hope to ride fast. His next entry was in East Germany at the Sachsenring, near Karl-Marx Stadt, formerly known as Chemnitz, not far from Dresden, on the other side of the Iron Curtain. It was a long and tedious journey, and the start money paid partly in local currency was minimal. But to make a name and start building a track record, a rider had no choice. Jack was again entered in both classes, but did not finish either race.

We don't know much more about that first 1958 season. Jack must have had a tough time but, on several occasions during his career, he said that he knew

The paddocks of the '50s and '60s were a jumble of vehicles: motorbikes, cars, and vans that provided accommodation and workshop space.

what to expect, and that first year in England did not reduce his determination to succeed.

What followed confirms this as, after spending a winter working hard in England, Jack bought a second Manx Norton, this time a genuine 500. In April 1959, he entered in two classes at Silverstone, without any convincing results. At the beginning of May, he was in Salzburg, Austria, where he finished seventh in the 350. A week later, he raced at Zandvoort in Holland, finishing fifth twice. There, he met Bob West, another Australian, who was there as a spectator to help friends. He was a racer himself, but had gone to Europe without any bikes, to get the lie of the land, ready to give a hand here and there to anyone in need. He and Jack immediately got along well and became friends. So much so that, later on, having found work and rented a house in Birmingham, West suggested Jack and Eileen go to live with him to share expenses.

The goal of all the riders then was to compete in the Grand Prix races that counted for the World Championship, the most prestigious but also the toughest to compete in. There were about ten such races each year but, to get a start in them, riders had to make a name for themselves by racing in the myriad international races, meeting each Sunday in various corners of Europe. Once they were accepted into a Grand Prix they had to finish among the top six to score points for the World Championship. This required long trips by truck or van to transport the motorcycles, a nomadic life lacking any comfort. None of this deterred those men, all driven by the same passion, enjoying travelling together and meeting up each week in an improvised paddock set up beside a local road turned into a racing circuit for two days.

So, little by little, a track record was established as a name became known. After

Zandvoort, at Tubbergen, still in Holland, Jack took fourth place in the 500, and the name Findlay was mentioned in a newspaper. Spectators noticed him, organisers remembered him, and gradually the start money improved. For each race, riders had to negotiate a price. The first letter asked for an entry in the race, then a second followed asking for better start money, and inevitably from one year to the next an organiser favoured riders he found likeable – Jack was always one of those.

Meanwhile, there were the must-attend events: the Tourist Trophy on the Isle of Man was the queen of races, the hardest, most expensive and most dangerous, too. Jack immediately fell in love with this 60km loop starting from Douglas, following the west coast to the north of the island, going from sea level to nearly the summit of Mount Snaefell at 621 metres (2037ft), with all the high-speed challenges a rider faced, before descending back to Douglas. At the TT, you didn't start in a group: you raced against yourself before racing against others. Jack loved this, the solitude he experienced on a long circuit, the solitary quest for the absolute success. Even though his first two races there ended in retirement, he returned there each year for nearly 20 years. The 1959 Senior TT was frustrating: he was 12th when he had to retire on the last lap.

Good finishes at Zandvoort and Tubbergen opened the door to entries for the Dutch TT at the Assen circuit, the Grand Prix of Holland, the most difficult race to get a start in. The organisers were ruthless, raising the bar to ensure only the best riders in the world were on their starting grid. The circuit was long and technical, the finishing places fiercely contested. Jack did not finish either race, but now he knew the layout of the Van Drenthe circuit.

John Tickle, a rider Jack met racing in England, suggested they compete together in the Barcelona 24 Hours in Spain, an endurance race on the Montjuich Park circuit; tortuous and dangerous, running uphill and downhill in the centre of the city. Their motorcycle was a 125 Montesa. Despite an honourable ninth place, Jack drew two conclusions: first, he didn't like endurance races, and also such a small-displacement bike was of no interest to him. This did not prevent him from competing in other such races or riding 125s again, but it was always without any pleasure or conviction.

After Spain, he went to Sweden and Kristianstad, without any results. At the Ulster Grand Prix at Dundrod in Northern Ireland, he finished ninth in the 500. Then, more meetings in England, at Snetterton, Aintree, Scarborough and Mallory Park. The start money was miserable, often non-existent, although prize money was a bit better. To earn that, however, you had to rub elbows with all the madmen racing there all the time.

Nevertheless, the 1959 season was far more profitable than the previous one, with nearly 20 meetings competed at in two categories, including three World Championship events, and many new circuits memorised. This was the schooling of the Continental Circus, hard and demanding, with the objective not necessarily to live off racing, but at least to make it more or less profitable, and above all to reach the holy grail of winning a Grand Prix counting for the World Championship.

Helmet, you say?

The riders' helmets have always acted as a distinctive badge, identifying the man and bearing information, such as asserting a nationality. Moreover, in the interwar period, during the European Championship era, it was accepted that white represented the Germans, green the English, red the Italians, and blue the French, even though not everyone adhered to this custom.

In the '50s and '60s, as motorcycle racing developed throughout Europe, organisers always sought to feature riders from distant countries, to add an exotic touch to the line-up. When there was a fight at the front, commentators rarely mentioned the riders' names, but referred to them as the Australian, the South African, or the Italian, who the Frenchman inevitably came to challenge. Helmets became, more than ever, an effective means of visual communication, with recognisable emblems: kangaroos for the Aussies, kiwis for the New Zealanders, springboks for the South Africans. This was, of course, more understandable than a national emblem or flag. Mike Duff's maple leaf was not always perceived as a symbol of Canada, nor Geoff Duke's red rose as his regional Lancashire emblem.

Over the years Jack's small white kangaroo on a blue background became an icon of its own, so strongly did it identify him. His kangaroo, with its back almost horizontal from head to tail, stood out from all the others. When Jack changed helmets, he carefully cut out a small kangaroo from a sheet of white sticker, always using the same small cardboard template that he carefully guarded. That's why, if you compare the helmets he wore during his different periods in racing, his kangaroo signature never varied.

Top to bottom: Jack Findlay's kangaroo, Hugh Anderson's kiwi, and Paddy Driver's springbok.

CHAPTER 2

Conquering Europe

England, 1960-1962

For the 1960 season, Jack kept the 500 Manx he'd bought a year earlier, and acquired a new 350 to replace the older one. His friend, Bob West, who'd found a good job in England, bought two Manx Nortons on which to try his luck at European circuits. The two friends decided to pool their resources for the season to make their adventure more cost-effective. They managed to acquire a practical truck tall enough to install bunks above the bikes.

Bob, who passed away in 2009, shared some memories of that time with Don Cox. "Jack helped me a lot that season, teaching me all the tricks to get entries, sending all those letters to organisers to get start money. We did a bunch of races together, including in the Eastern bloc where it was easy to get entries, and we made the most of it. But we travelled a lot, too, going from Holland to Yugoslavia with a detour in Austria to get visas, then heading quickly to another country. It was really a great season. When I returned to Australia, when I raced in local meetings I achieved my best results there, thanks to that experience in Europe."

The 1960 season started for Jack with a few meetings in England and on the Continent. After two respectable finishes in Mettet, Belgium, he attended the French Grand Prix in Clermont-Ferrand, where a series of incidents would profoundly influence his life. This first GP of the season was supposed to be a chance to get noticed, but after achieving the third fastest time in 350 practice, behind John Surtees' MV Agusta and Franta Stastny on a Jawa, Jack crashed at the end of the session and ended up in a ravine. What should have been just a bad memory led to a double encounter that changed the course of his career.

After his fall, while waiting to be evacuated to the Clermont-Ferrand Hospital,

Jack with his South African friend Paddy Driver at Albi in 1962.

the organisers searched the paddock for someone to act as an interpreter between him and the doctors. Nanou, the partner of Jacques Insermini, the French champion entered in the race, volunteered. Her real name was Andrée Lyonnard. She had been with Insermini for several years and spoke perfect English. She accompanied Jack to the hospital where, after lengthy discussions, the doctors agreed to discharge

The four Manx Nortons of Jack Findlay and Bob West at the beginning of the 1960 season.

him because Jack was determined to race the next day. This was a bad idea and, after a few laps, feeling dizzy, he wisely decided to pull in, ending a Grand Prix that had been a fiasco for him.

However, this incident led to a close friendship between Insermini, Nanou and Jack, who from then on spent a lot of time together. The French rider had an apartment in the very centre of Paris, and the use of his father's house in Saint-Raphaël, on the coast of the Var region of Provence. Insermini was not an ordinary man: as a youth, he competed in athletics, wrestling and weightlifting, even being part of the French team in these different disciplines. He was a force of nature and an

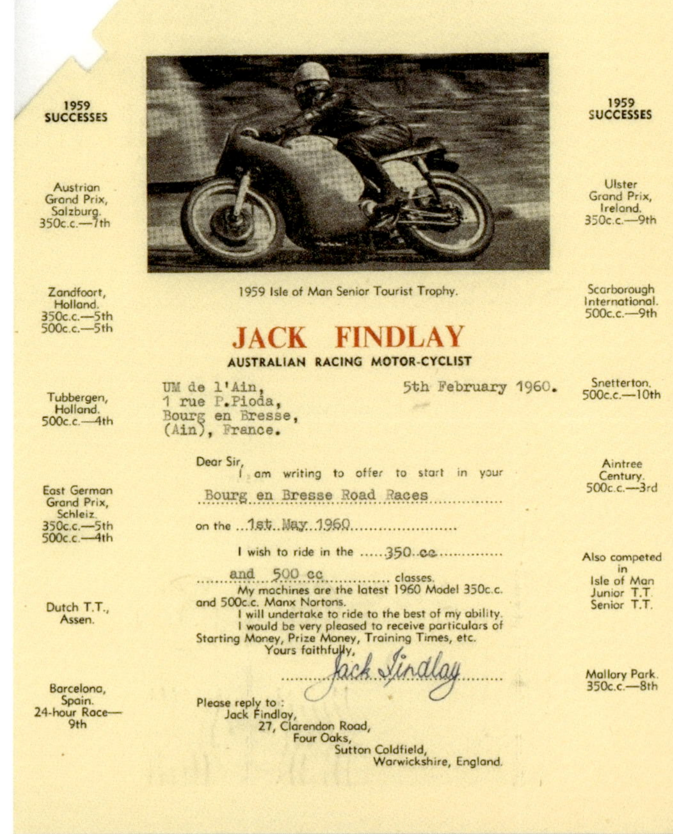

1959 SUCCESSES

Austrian Grand Prix, Salzburg. 350c.c.—7th

Zandfoort, Holland. 350c.c.—5th 500c.c.—5th

Tubbergen, Holland. 500c.c.—4th

East German Grand Prix, Schleiz. 350c.c.—5th 500c.c.—4th

Dutch T.T., Assen.

Barcelona, Spain. 24-hour Race—9th

1959 Isle of Man Senior Tourist Trophy.

JACK FINDLAY
AUSTRALIAN RACING MOTOR-CYCLIST

UM de l'Ain,
1 rue P.Pioda,
Bourg en Bresse,
(Ain), France.

5th February 1960.

Dear Sir,
I am writing to offer to start in your Bourg en Bresse Road Races
on the 1st May 1960
I wish to ride in the 350 cc and 500 cc classes.
My machines are the latest 1960 Model 350c.c. and 500c.c. Manx Nortons.
I will undertake to ride to the best of my ability.
I would be very pleased to receive particulars of Starting Money, Prize Money, Training Times, etc.
Yours faithfully,
Jack Findlay

Please reply to :
Jack Findlay,
27, Clarendon Road,
Four Oaks,
Sutton Coldfield,
Warwickshire, England.

1959 SUCCESSES

Ulster Grand Prix, Ireland. 350c.c.—9th

Scarborough International. 500c.c.—9th

Snetterton. 500c.c.—10th

Aintree Century. 500c.c.—3rd

Also competed in Isle of Man Junior T.T. Senior T.T.

Mallory Park. 350c.c.—8th

In 1960, Jack's letters look fine, but his results are yet to get better.

Jack at the Sachsenring in 1960, then a non-World Championship race.

accomplished sportsman. He was a trained mechanic who started racing by chance on a bike he prepared for a friend, who loaned it to him when he couldn't take part in a race himself. Quickly, Insermini became one of the top French motorcycle racers, winning several French championships. In 1957, through Jacques Collot, his friend and on-track rival who was also a French champion, he met Nanou, an energetic and independent woman who shared his life for nearly seven years. Having lived in the US, she spoke perfect English, helping to strengthen ties between Insermini and many English-speaking riders. "My apartment in Paris and the house in Saint-Raphaël became places to stay for many riders," said Insermini. "Paddy Driver, Rob Fitton, Bob Brown, Ralph Rensen or Mike Hailwood would often come to sleep at my place. One summer, half a dozen trucks were in the villa's garden in the south of France. The guys had taken out the bikes and pitched their tents there."

After their meeting, Jack became a regular at their Paris apartment. He even used it as his mailing address and, later, due to its proximity to the headquarters of the French Motorcycle Federation, he obtained a French licence.

After his fall at the Charade circuit and this decisive meeting, Jack continued his tour of European race circuits with Bob West, relentlessly criss-crossing the continent from Germany to Holland, Austria, Yugoslavia and Italy, achieving good results here and there, which allowed him to compete in more Grand Prix races. He raced in the World Championship GP races in the Isle of Man, Holland, Belgium and Germany, but each time it was a struggle with the organisers – convincing them to give a start to a young rider was far from easy. After the Ulster GP, Jack managed to get an entry for the Italian GP at Monza. Finishing eighth in the 500 race secured starts for the following season in Italy, where people had started talking about him.

In total, that 1960 season included about 20 meetings and nearly 40 starts; Jack was now fully immersed in the Continental Circus. But at the end of it, Bob West decided to leave England. "It was exciting to discover Europe and all those circuits, but the moment I realised it wasn't for me was during the Belgian GP at Spa. I'd made a pit stop during the race, and the leaders passed me just as I rejoined the circuit. After following them for a while, I realised that if I had to ride like that all the time to have any hopes of winning, I'd rather go back home to Australia. So I did!"

Four shots from the 1960 French GP in Clermont-Ferrand. Left: Jack qualified in third spot in the 350 race after a crash in practice. Bottom left: Jack on the starting grid beside John Surtees' MV Agusta (1), Franta Stastny's Jawa (39) and Paddy Driver's Norton (17). Above: Tea time for Jack, his friend Bob West and their mechanic. Below: Jack was safe after his crash in practice. Still sore, he withdrew from the race after a few laps.

As soon as they met, Jack Findlay became friends with French rider Jacques Insermini. Here they are beside Nanou and Australian rider Jack Ahearn at the Pau prize-giving in 1961

By contrast, Jack was more determined than ever. At the start of the 1961 season, he benefitted from the help and advice of an Irish rider, Ralph Rensen. They already know each other, but their friendship solidified at Pau during the first meeting of the season in France. They put on a show in both the 350 and 500 classes, and although Jack crashed in the larger capacity race after finishing just behind Rensen in the 350, his performance was noted by the French press. Eight days later, they met again on the long Le Mans circuit, the 13km (8 miles) one used for the 24-hour car race, famous for its 6km (3.75 miles) Mulsanne Straight. Again, they put on a show, Rensen winning one race and Jack the other, his first victory in a major International race.

"Actually, Rensen almost quit racing at the end of the previous year, because he was deeply affected by Dave Chadwick's death in April 1960 at Mettet," Jacques Insermini, who knew them both well, recounted. "It was a terrible shock for me too: they had all stayed at my Paris apartment before heading to Belgium. Chadwick's wife, who had a baby, preferred to stay in Paris to rest. I had to break the terrible news to her when I returned from Mettet. We all experienced moments like that; losing a friend was always testing. Rensen was very upset, but during the winter he got an offer from the Bultaco factory to ride their new 125s, and that convinced him to continue for another season."

After their successes at Le Mans and Pau, Rensen and Findlay were the favourites when they arrived in Bourg-en-Bresse. They dominated both races, together with Insermini, the French champion. Rensen won twice, and Jacques and Jack shared the podium places, the Australian taking second in the 350 but having to settle for third in the 500.

In recalling those days, Insermini revealed some secrets about those men who met on the track every Sunday. "Racing was our passion, but it was horribly dangerous, and several of us lost their lives each year. So, when we were among friends, guys we trusted, we agreed before the race to put on a show for the public, battling lap after lap, and only really competing for victory in the last two or three laps. Open-road circuits had so many obstacles – walls, trees, poles – that it was foolish to take every risk throughout the race from start to finish. When we did that, the public wasn't cheated, the winner won fair and square, and it boosted our ratings with the organisers, who would pay us better the following year."

This practice, confirmed by another great champion, Jim Redman, was a necessity for the brave men who sought to make their expensive passion as profitable as possible, while minimising risks. This didn't prevent a good number of dramas year after year, race after race.

"Racing was our passion, but it was horribly dangerous, and several of us lost their lives each year. "

Of course, that kind of arrangement couldn't happen during World Championship events, where the need to score points forced the riders to fight from start to finish, if necessary. Redman, who had the best machines from the Honda factory, still applied a personal rule: win races as slowly as possible. Easier said than done. Redman's career was filled with fierce battles on all circuits, including the most dangerous ones.

At the peak of this grim hierarchy was the Tourist Trophy, and during the 1961 edition, one of the victims was Ralph Rensen, who crashed fatally on the final lap of the Senior 500 race while in a good position. Two days earlier, he'd finished third in the Junior 350 race, showing that this demanding course spared neither seasoned riders nor beginners. For Jack it was a terrible blow, as, having crashed during the 350 race, he learned the news from a hospital bed in Douglas. This tragedy didn't make him question his passion for motorcycling and racing, but reinforced his solitary nature. "What's the point of making friends who can die at any moment?" he often declared in interviews afterwards.

Since the show had to go on, the litany of races lengthened; International meetings with easy races alternated with World Championship events where the competition was tough. But tenacity paid off. After an eighth place at the Belgian

Even a fair dice between friends can end badly, as Jacques Insermini crashes in Pau in 1961.

In the early weeks of the 1961 season, Jack was helped by Irish ace Ralph Rensen.

Jack and Rensen side-by-side in Pau, where they dominated both 350 and 500cc races.

Grand Prix, Jack headed east, finishing fifth on his 500 at the Sachsenring in East Germany, earning his first World Championship points. Then it was back to the UK to race at Oulton Park, and then to the Ulster GP. The season drew to a close with a final Grand Prix at Monza in Italy. In finishing sixth in the 500 after a fierce battle with Frank Perris and Karl Hoppe, Jack earned an additional point, securing 16th position in the final standings. He was now firmly established among the best-known riders of the Continental Circus, making it easier to secure entries, and negotiate better start money.

Les trois champions. De gauche à droite : Mike Hailwood, Jacques Insermieri et Jack Fonley. (Photo Ph. Laudon)

An amusing cutting from a local French newspaper talking about Mike Hailwood and Jack's visit to Jacques Insermini's house in Saint-Raphaël on the French Riviera.

In November, knowing how to attract attention when the season was over, Jacques Insermini suggested Jack joined him in an attempt to break world records over 1000km and six hours at the Montlhéry circuit near Paris, using his 500 Manx Norton with its engine prepared by Reg Dearden. The bike was fitted with a full fairing, and the two riders practised for several days despite the bad weather, which delayed the attempt. On the day they set off, everything went well at first; the bike and its riders easily reached an average of 202km/h (125.5mph), and the record was in sight. But things went awry after the halfway point. During a stint where Jack was in the saddle, a rear shock absorber rod broke under the stresses of the bumpy concrete bankings. He struggled to stay upright as the bike zigzagged at speed, and fortunately he managed to control it. No

RECORDS

Jean Murit convoite à nouveau le record des 24 heures. Après l'avoir porté de 136,550 à 155,267 kmh avec une B.M.W., une Velocette préparée par l'usine anglaise lui fit passer le cap des 100 miles par heure (161,009 kmh); record qu'une équipe britannique, M.L.G., devait une semaine plus tard accrocher à 175,806 kmh. Jean Murit ne s'avoue pas battu, et c'est pour prendre sa revanche qu'il a préparé cette B.M.W. R 50 S de 500 cc.

On notera la finesse du carénage, celui-là même que Insermini et Findlay montèrent sur leur Norton pour leur infructueuse tentative. L'Australien Jack Findlay et le champion de France Jacques Insermini que l'on voit ici en compagnie de Murit, compteront parmi les pilotes de cette tentative au succès problématique.

Il faut se souvenir que Reg Dearden, le metteur au point de Manchester bien connu, s'y cassa les dents voici un an ! D'autre part, G. Monneret a l'intention de battre, toujours sur 24 h., les records 50 cc (Vap) et 125 cc (Morini).

De gauche à dr.: Insermini, Findlay, Murit.

A press report of Jack and Insermini's record attempt on a 500 BMW prepared by French sidecar champion Jean Murit.

Top picture: Each race can be an adventure! Jack has just crashed at the Forest Hairpin in Bourg-en-Bresse in 1962.

Above: A proud Jack with the McIntyre-framed 500 Matchless he had just brought back to Paris at the end of 1962.

records were broken, but there were favourable articles in the press, which was never to be dismissed. In fact, the two men returned to Montlhéry for another attempt in March 1962, but that time with a BMW provided and prepared by Jean Murit, the former French sidecar champion, who had become the German brand's largest dealer in Paris.

The 1961 season was fruitful, not only on the tracks. In August, Eileen gave birth to a baby boy. Jack chose his names: Gregory Ralph, in memory of two friends lost in racing. To end the year, the young couple and their baby returned to Australia to visit their families. But, a few weeks later, when it was time to return to England on the eve of the 1962 season, Jack arrived alone. Tired of the English winter, of a country where she knew no one, and of the uncertain life that did not suit her, Eileen decided to stay in Australia with the baby. It was a tough blow for Jack, who could barely cope with the break-up, and would never mention this son of his in the decades to come.

When he returned to Europe, his only close friends were Jacques Insermini and his partner, Nanou, in Paris. That's when he decided to settle in France, where Insermini's apartment became his base and postal address. The French champion knew the small competition scene in Paris well. Everything was easier to find, whether a workshop, suppliers or people capable of remaking or repairing parts.

After deciding to establish his base in Paris, to give himself every chance, Jack went to England to buy two brand-new Manx Norton motorcycles. For the first time, the Australian federation honoured him with the status of representative of Australia for the Isle of Man Tourist Trophy, with a little money attached. The 1962 season looked promising. But in racing, you can never be sure of anything.

As early as mid-February, Jack raced in Málaga in southern Spain, where he won one race and was second in the other. Later, in a 500 race in Le Mans, he finished fifth. Then came two second places in Pau but, from May on, a series of mechanical failures demoralised him and left his efforts unrewarded. Race after race, breakdowns accumulated while Jack still fought among the leaders. One day it was the magneto, another the gearbox. Most often it was a valve that broke. "I felt cursed: I broke an exhaust valve several times." As a result, there were two retirements at the Tourist Trophy and at Assen, the two most important GPs of the season. A fifth place at the Belgian GP in Spa saved face and gave him two points, but it was not enough to lift his spirits. The bad luck pursued him until the very end of the season, with a final retirement in the Italian GP at Monza.

Jack and Jacques Insermini with their Norton prepared for record attempts in Montlhéry at the end of 1961.

Perhaps it was this series of breakdowns that prompted Insermini to declare: "One of Jack's shortcomings at the time was that he wasn't very good at mechanics. He could do a lot of things, but he lacked the consistency for fine tuning. Setting up a Norton Manx's cam drive has always been tricky. Everything became simpler when he changed engines for the Matchless."

This welcome change took place at the end of the 1962 season, this time by sheer good fortune. Jack was at rock bottom. He had tested a Formula 1 car and was thinking of switching to four wheels, or even giving everything up to return to live in Australia and find a job there. His salvation would come from Lew Ellis, the competition manager of the Shell Oil company in England, who took a liking to him. Ellis encouraged him to continue racing motorcycles, gave him financial assistance, and even negotiated the purchase of Bob McIntyre's 500 Matchless for him. This great Scottish champion had had this bike built at the beginning of 1962, but hardly used it as he was under contract with the Honda factory. He suffered a fatal accident at the Oulton Park circuit in August that year, hence the sale of this bike. Jack went to fetch it in England at the end of November.

On his return to Paris, he invited French photographer friends to shoot it, posing with a machine that carried all his hopes. The frame had been created by Alex Crummie, a friend of McIntyre's, who designed it to be equipped with a 500 Matchless G50 or 350 AJS 7R engine, very similar in design to one another. The bike's equipment was still pretty basic when Jack acquired it, but he'd continue to improve it later. As he posed with his new mount in the courtyard of his Parisian workshop, Jack was happy to be turning a new page. And not just for him: his friend Jacques Insermini decided to end his own motorcycle racing career. He wouldn't stop competing, as he would race on four wheels in rallying, behind the wheel of a factory Lancia. His decision led to another: his girlfriend, Nanou, who was really passionate about life in the motorcycle paddock where she had all her friends, decided to follow Jack in his two-wheel career. "It was logical that she didn't stay with me," Insermini said later. "I got along well with Nanou, but she was really in love with bike racing and the Continental Circus. It was her life. With Jack, she could continue this adventure even better than with me."

It was called the Continental Circus

From spring to autumn, motorcycle races were organised all over Europe, mostly on improvised circuits, on roads closed to traffic. Sunday after Sunday, races were held in England, France, Germany, the Netherlands, or any other country, including those beyond the Iron Curtain, such as East Germany, Czechoslovakia and Yugoslavia. In the Grand Prix events, the top six finishers earned points towards the World Championship (8-6-4-3-2-1 based on the finishing order). The riders led a nomadic life, travelling from one race to another with their small truck or van carrying their bikes and the essential equipment for racing. Each time, they had to negotiate start money on the basis of their track record or reputation, which was built up race after race, with the most renowned being the Grand Prix events counting towards the World Championships. But the spots were precious, both on the starting grid and at the finish.

Like showmen travelling from town to town, the riders slept in the paddocks and moved on to another venue as soon as the races were over. This migration was called the Continental Circus, and the most famous riders became emblematic of it. It's considered that the Continental Circus existed in its most classic form from 1955 to 1985 because, afterwards, the teams strengthened and organised themselves within an association, and the organisation of the races came under the control of a promoter, to whom the FIM, the international federation, delegated the management of high-level motorcycle sport.

Jack on his very unreliable 350 Manx Norton.

At full speed during the 1962 Belgian GP in Spa.

The usual routine before a race – riders at technical scrutineering. Jack is beside Claude Lambert's sidecar.

CHAPTER 3

How to Make a Name for Yourself

1963-1965

During the winter of 1962-63, having sold his Manx Norton, Jack looked for a second ride to accompany the McIntyre G50. Nanou was by his side, providing efficient assistance in managing administrative issues. He could focus on the technical aspects. His choice was Benjamin Savoye's 250 Mondial – the French champion, a friend of Nanou's, had just retired from racing and was selling his bikes. As the French importer of this Italian brand, Savoye received factory assistance to obtain spare parts. It was an ex-works machine from the factory race team, which won the World Championship in 1958. Its single-cylinder engine with double overhead camshafts still seemed competitive. Jack took it for a spin at the Magny-Cours circuit in March, under the watchful eye of Savoye, who gave him advice. First outing, first victory. A week later, at Le Mans, he rode the McIntyre Matchless again, which he had raced in Málaga two weeks earlier, but without success due to ignition failure. At Le Mans, he triumphed masterfully, taking the lead after a few laps and never being caught. It's worth noting that he also started the 350 race with the 250 Mondial, and finished tenth.

After doing well at Cesenatico (fourth) and then at the Nürburgring (sixth), Jack suffered a fall at the Salzburgring on 1 May and injured his leg. Despite this, three days later he comfortably led the race at Bourg-en-Bresse with the 250 Mondial and set a new lap record, before a battery failure halted his momentum. Suffering from his injured leg, especially when pushing his bike at the start, he only managed eighth in the 500. As there was no 500 category at the German GP, Jack skipped it, preferring to head to Casablanca in Morocco, where he'd been offered a handsome start money deal. Two effortless victories justified this long journey via Spain and Gibraltar.

Jack riding his Mondial 250 at Bourg-en-Bresse in May 1963.

He was in Chimay, Belgium, 15 days later for another victory with the McIntyre Matchless. Next stop was the Isle of Man and its Tourist Trophy races.

To understand the life of these mechanised nomads, May 1963 is a telling example. Here's the extensive journey undertaken by Jack and Nanou: departure from Paris to Magny-Cours (300km), then to Le Mans (300km), Cesenatico on the Adriatic coast in Italy (1100km), the Nürburgring near Koblenz in Germany (1200km), Salzburg in Austria where the race took place on 1 May (500km), three days later Bourg-en-Bresse (900km), then a 15-day break to travel to Casablanca via Spain and Gibraltar (2200km), back up from Morocco to Chimay in Belgium (2800km), then the journey to the Tourist Trophy requiring two ferry crossings, first to England from France and then from Liverpool to Douglas (800km). As soon as the TT was over, they headed to Lyon (1000km), then back along the Italian

Jack about to race the Mondial 250 for the first time in Magny-Cours, helped by French champion Benjamin Savoye, who sold him the bike.

coast to Ospedaletti (1000km), then north again to Assen in the north of Holland (1200km).

Jack and Nanou covered 12,400km in five weeks, a distance with very few freeway stretches. This long journey resulted in two victories – in Casablanca, the 250 won easily, and the 500 after a fierce battle with Maurice Hawthorne, and another success with the Matchless at Chimay.

In the Isle of Man, for the Lightweight 250cc TT, Jack left his Mondial behind in favour of a more powerful DMW Hornet two-stroke loaned to him. By then, the category was dominated by a slew of Japanese machines from Honda, Yamaha and Suzuki. Spurred on by the spectators cheering for the British motorcycle, Jack was in sixth position at the end of the third lap when he crashed, fortunately without injury. The loan of a machine for the TT races would become a habit over the years. In Britain, sponsors and tuners were numerous. Many had just one or two machines that they lent out for various races to the rider of their choice. In their eyes, Jack was in demand, and from the 1963 season onwards, it would always be easy for him to borrow bikes to race in Britain, mainly at the TT.

Good results followed in International meetings, with third places at Ospedaletti and Mettet, for example, but the Grand Prix rounds were much more complicated. Firstly, the races were much longer, 180 to 200km (110 to 120 miles), whereas the non-championship International races were run over distances of about 100km (60 miles). Secondly, in GPs, the level of competition was higher, in terms of men and machines. Only the first six over the finish line scored points that counted towards the final World Championship standings, and to achieve that, they needed a fast, reliable bike and a skilled rider capable of going the distance.

The Mondial 250 beside the Matchless 500 in the Le Mans paddock in 1963.

Jack was again on a British two-stroke single, this time the 250 Cotton at Assen for the Dutch TT, where he suffered the bitterness of two retirements. At Spa, for the Belgian GP, he rode the Mondial again, by then equipped with dual ignition, making it both slightly more reliable and faster. On the Matchless, he tried a six-speed Schafleitner gearbox, but it didn't fit easily into the McIntyre frame. He switched back to the four-speed AMC gearbox for the race, but still managed to fight with the leading group until he had to stop to refuel. That's a tough lesson: Spa was the fastest

For the Dutch TT in June, Jack was racing the DMW 250 he'd previously ridden in the Isle of Man.

JACK FINDLAY

AUSTRALIA

59 Rue Montmartre,
Paris, 2e.
5. 3. 1963.

Union Motocycliste de l'Ain,
1 Rue Paul Pioda,
Bourg-en-Bresse, (Ain).

Monsieur le Président,

Désirant participer à votre"Circuit de Vitesse International Bourg-en-Bresse", du 5.5.1963 je vous serais reconnaissant de bien vouloir me faire parvenir des bulletins d'engagements pour 2 catégories, ainsi que le reglement.

Je me permet de vous suggerer une prime de départ de 90,000 Frs., car je possède la 500cc "Speciale Bob MacIntyre" Matchless, avec le moteur d'usine, ainsi que la 250cc Mondial.

En attendant une réponse que j'éspère favorable, je vous prie d'agreer Monsieur le Président mes respectueuses salutations.

Jack Findlay,

Jack Findlay.

Reçue le: 8-3-63
Répondue le: 28 MAR 1963
Régl. expédié:
Eng. reçu:
Hôtel:

1962 Successes.

1st. Chimay, Belgium, 350cc (Lap Record).
1st. Chimay, Belgium, 500cc.
1st. Malaga, Spain, 350cc.
2nd. San Remo, Italy, 500cc.
2nd. Pau, France, 350cc.
2nd. Pau, France, 500cc.
2nd. Malaga, Spain, 500cc.
3rd. Mettet, Belgium, 350cc.
4th. Nurburgring, Germany, 350cc.
5th. Belgian Grand Prix, Francorchamps, 500cc.
5th. St. Wendel, Saar, 500cc.
5th. Le Mans, France, 500cc.
6th. Le Mans, France, 350cc (Lap Record).

1961 Successes.

2nd. Le Mans, France, 500cc.
2nd. Pau, France, 350cc.
2nd. Vesoul, France, 500cc.
2nd. Bourg-en-Bresse, France, 350cc.
3rd. Czechoslovakia Grand Prix, Brno, 500cc.
3rd. Austrian Grand Prix, Salzburg, 500cc.
3rd. Jicin, Czechoslovakia, 350cc.
3rd. Jicin, Czechoslovakia, 500cc.
3rd. Bourg-en-Bresse, France, 500cc.
4th. St. Wendel, Saar, 500cc.
5th. East German Grand prix, Sachsenring, 500cc.
6th. Italian Grand Prix, Monza, 500cc.
7th. Italian Grand Prix, Monza, 350cc.

In 1963, Jack's book of successes was bigger, so he could advertise several victories.

circuit of all, with an average speed of 200km/h (125mph), so fuel consumption was very high. The unexpected pit stop was a huge frustration for Jack, who loved this track where the long, open curves are taken at frightening speed.

A paradox that began in the early '60s would follow Jack throughout his career: he was well liked and appreciated in Britain, but he didn't particularly enjoy English circuits. The two temples of speed there are Brands Hatch and Mallory Park, ultra-short circuits of around 2km (1.25 miles) in length, where equally short races with qualifying heats took place all in one day. Jack hated this system all the more because there was little or no start money to pay expenses, only prize money. That's why, throughout his career, he would rarely be seen on British circuits, except when one race or another was on the way to the two Grand Prix events held there, namely the Isle of Man TT in June, or the Ulster GP in August. After returning from the TT, it was easy to race at Mallory Park to satisfy a sponsor. For the Ulster, there was usually a race at Oulton Park eight days before or after. Moreover, the layout of Oulton Park, at nearly 5km (3 miles) long, was more similar to continental circuits than the Mallory Park merry-go-round. On the way to the Ulster, Jack finished fourth there on the 500 Matchless. At Dundrod, he was battling with Mike Duff and Fred Stevens for third place when he crashed. Fortunately, a fifth place at the Sachsenring circuit a week later brought him two points in the World Championship, consoling him for this mishap.

A rare picture of Jack riding his Matchless G50 at the Montlhéry circuit near Paris.

Front row for the 1963 Italian GP in Monza. Jack is closest to the camera on the lone single beside Hailwood's MV four, Minter and Read's Gilera fours and Venturi's Bianchi twin.

A first Grand Prix podium for Jack, beside Mike Hailwood at the 1963 Italian round in Monza.

A fun race in Casablanca (Morocco) in October 1963 for Tom Kirby's three riders: Jack (79), Driver (80) and Hailwood (81).

To please Savoye, and to confirm his growing closeness to France since Nanou had been accompanying him, Jack took part in two National events, one at Albi just before the Italian Grand Prix, and another in Montlhéry outside Paris shortly after. A victory in Albi in the 250 class and another at Montlhéry in the 500 race improved his best result so far in a World Championship race, a brilliant second place on the Monza circuit in the Italian Grand Prix. With its sweeping curves, similar to Spa, this ultra-fast but demanding track also became one of his favourites. From there, the final European race in Zaragoza, Spain, allowed a stopover before a second race in Morocco, bearing the title of the Casablanca Grand Prix, where they would meet up with friends.

During that summer, the famous British sponsor Tom Kirby announced he would strengthen his Grand Prix race team, and that Jack would be part of that, alongside South African Paddy Driver, in the 350 and 500 classes. To complete the celebration, Kirby decided to enter three bikes in the Casablanca Grand Prix. Mike Hailwood, the undisputed 500cc world champion on his four-cylinder MV Agusta, joined Jack and Driver, using one of Tom Kirby's Matchless bikes for the occasion. The field was well stocked, with the notable presence of the great French champion Georges Monneret, for whom this would be one of his last races, after a career spanning nearly 30 years. The race lived up to its promises with a fierce battle for victory, with everyone eager to challenge Hailwood, who for once was on an equal footing in terms of machinery. Nevertheless, he won with his usual flair, ahead of Driver and Jack.

For the first time since embarking on the great adventure, Jack finished the year satisfied. He was eighth in the 500cc World Championship with eight points, and he scored eight race victories in International non-title events.

The same as in the previous year, Jack decided to spend the winter in Paris with Nanou. They lived in the apartment belonging to Insermini, who was often away. Located in the heart of Paris, it was within walking distance of the offices of the French Motorcycle Federation, as well as the only French motorcycle magazine, *Moto*

The left side of the McIntyre G50 in Spa, with a windshield toward the rear of the frame.

Top: Jack with the McIntyre-framed AJS 350 at Bourg-en-Bresse in 1964.

Centre: Jack leads fellow Aussie Dennis Fry and Swede Esso Gunnarsson.

Bottom: Jack at the 1964 East German GP at the Sachsenring. His McIntyre Matchless used a bulky two-part Jakeman fairing.

Revue. Jack would also obtain a French licence "because," he explained, "their insurance system was better than the British ACU's."

Nanou naturally reinforced her role as secretary for all race paperwork. She maintained good relations with many organisers, many of whom were charmed by her, as well as some journalists, which helped garner attention for Jack. Thanks to Insermini, who put him in touch with his networks in the motorcycle and automobile industries, Jack was able to find a nearby workshop to prepare his bikes, to such an extent that, in the months to come, through contacts at the Matra factory, he was able to have special parts made, including a titanium con rod for his Matchless G50's 500cc engine.

Although assured of Tom Kirby's financial and logistic support, Jack wanted to race with his own bikes. Having become accustomed to the McIntyre chassis, at the end of the 1963 season he had a new frame built, an exact copy with one difference: it was slightly wider. As for the original frame, he installed a 350cc AJS engine in it prepared by Kirby.

"I really wanted to combine my engine with a new five-speed gearbox, but the lower loop of the frame was too narrow, and it would have required major modifications," said Jack. "I preferred to have a second frame built in England by Bill Jakeman, to allow fitting the five-speed gearbox. I still called this bike a McIntyre Matchless, but strictly speaking it was no longer the one designed and built by him – it was my bike. As it was low and narrow, Bill Jakeman designed and made a very slim fairing. I had a large tank made, adapted to the length of the Grand Prix races."

As in previous years, Jack rode a Villiers-engined 250 DMW in the 1965 250 Isle of Man Lightweight TT race.

Everything seemed to be going well for the man now nicknamed the 'Australian from Paris'.

In 1964, Jack planned to compete again in the 350 and 500 classes. But as good news never comes alone, the DMW factory announced it wanted to hire him again for the Lightweight TT in the Isle of Man, to ride its 250 single. All this confirmed his status as a truly professional rider.

The season began with the US Grand Prix held on the Daytona Speedway infield course surrounded by the steep bankings. Tom Kirby sent three of his machines – for Paddy Driver, Phil Read and Jack, who encountered only trouble, both in practice and the race. Barely back from the US, everyone met up again on the Adriatic coast in Italy. Before the first GP of the season, meetings were held there at quite a rate. In Rimini or Cesenatico, the roads along the seaside promenade turned into improvised circuits. The riders were treated like kings, as guests of hotels and restaurants eager to welcome them. Moreover, the start money was excellent, to the extent that some riders preferred these events to the Grands Prix, where the organisers took advantage of the fact they needed to score World Championship points in their events to pay them poorly. The World

Mystery bike: Jack on a 250 Yamaha-engined machine at the Sachsenring in 1965.

Championships were contested in six categories catering for 50, 125, 250, 250, and 500cc solos plus 500cc sidecars, but organisers didn't always include all categories in their race programme. When a rider could only do one race at a GP, they prioritised doing a second class with a smaller-capacity bike without being competitive, so they could race twice that weekend and collect double the start money.

"Jack really had faith ... every penny earned was invested in racing. It was the same for all the riders, fuelled by passion and the pleasure of competing. But it really was living life on the edge."

In the first race in Italy at Modena, Jack's friend Mike Hailwood played a nasty trick on him by banging into him while they were battling for the lead. Two good results at Cervia (second) and Imola (seventh) consoled him. From there, it was Salzburg (third in 350), then Bourg-en-Bresse (fourth in 350) but, alas, a retirement due to a battery failure in the 500. Then it was off to the UK, with two podiums at the Northern Irish North West 200 (third and second), and then the Tourist Trophy, where the competition was tough. Thirteenth in the Senior race was barely acceptable. In fact, the new McIntyre G50 was not yet perfectly adapted to Jack: the fairing was not entirely satisfactory, with the ignition and gearbox temperamental. As for the 350, its AJS 7R engine prepared by Tom Kirby proved more fragile than its big brother, the G50 Matchless. Jack managed to score points in Belgium, with a fine fifth place (500), and after a series of adequately fruitful non-championship races, he concluded his GP season with another fifth place at Monza (500). Just to round it off, in the last race of the year in Zaragoza, Spain, he conceded the 500 victory to Gyula Marsovski after a stern battle.

Jack on the 350 McIntyre AJS at Ballaugh Bridge during the 1965 Junior TT.

In the end, the 1964 season produced mixed fortunes for Jack. He was 14th overall in the 500 World Championship with four points, thanks to his two fifth places in Belgium and Italy. In the 350, he didn't finish many races, and didn't score any points in GPs. Tom Kirby's support didn't bring the expected results, thanks to his engines being so fragile. Jack felt frustrated to see that all the efforts he made were so poorly rewarded. Certainly, he managed to make a living from his racing, but each season relied on a fragile balance between start money and prize money, machine loans and small product support – some tyres here, a few sparkplugs or oil there. His only small financial contract was with the Shell Oil company.

Jack follows Walter Scheimann over the old Salzburg circuit's cobblestones.

"Jack really had faith," Nanou told me. "All these years have been really tough; every penny earned was invested in racing. It was the same for all the riders, fuelled by passion and the pleasure of competing. But it really was living life on the edge."

Reflecting on his 1964 season, Jack confided in me: "Every season was new, everything had to be rethought. In 1963, I had an excellent year, in terms of wins and honourable finishes. Due to the unreliability of my machines, especially the 350, the following season was less good. For 1965, I decided to reorganise myself by making the 500 my No.1 priority. I knew that Tom Kirby and Bill Jakeman would continue to help me, but I needed to find other sponsors."

So, after England, Jack turned to Italy, where the motorcycle industry was filled

Jack on his 350 McIntyre AJS leading Paddy Driver on his Kirby AJS at the Sachsenring in 1965.

Jack on his 500 bike at La Source hairpin on the Spa circuit in 1964.

with life. In 1962, he had mounted an Oldani brake on his Norton, which he had kept on the 350 McIntyre AJS. To improve the braking of the 500, while seeking out new contacts in Milan, he met Daniele Fontana. He was a passionate man who had just started making competition brakes. Born in 1927, almost ten years older than Jack, Fontana was a lively person who led a peculiar life. As a child, he followed his parents to Ethiopia during Mussolini's attempt at colonisation in the 1930s. After the war, back in Europe, he worked with an uncle in a Casino in Italy, and then in Monte Carlo. Returning to Italy, he set up a motorcycle repair shop, and tried his luck in competition, competing in rallies and races with a 175 Morini. Gradually, he equipped himself with machine tools, and his workshop gained a good reputation. One day, the Paton constructor Giuseppe Pattoni and his rider friend Gilberto Milani arrived to have their brakes relined. Fontana believed that the existing designs could be improved. He decided to create his own Fontana brand, and devoted himself entirely to this activity. His first such brake was ready in early '65. He needed a good test rider capable of being an ambassador for him on the race tracks. Jack was the ideal person for that.

When Jack went to the Fontana workshop for the first time, their encounter was almost love at first sight. "It was thanks to my motorcycle that I met Daniele Fontana, with whom I enjoyed the most beautiful friendship in my life. He helped me, we worked together, and of course, I always used his brakes on my motorcycles." The friendship would remain unwavering for more than ten years, until Daniele's sudden death from a heart attack in August 1976. Throughout that period, Fontana was a capable technical advisor and an important morale booster and financial supporter for Jack.

"Daniele was friends with everyone. Lots of engine tuners and race bike preparers came to see him, and they discussed all sorts of technical details. Through knowing them, he expanded his knowledge about all different engines, and especially knew everything about small Morini motors. And he knew everyone in the racing world in Italy." Hence, during the 1965 season, Jack started several races on a 125 Honda CR93 loaned by an Italian sponsor recommended by Fontana.

The contact with Fontana made everything easier in Italy. The passion for motorcycle racing was such that pilots were treated like demigods. It is no coincidence that in Italy, the word tifosi (ardent fans) was invented. There were many small manufacturers and accessory makers in Italy. There, you found the best boots, the best glasses and excellent components like forks, handlebars and brake

Start of the 500 race at Salzburg in 1965: Agostini (1) in front on his MV Agusta followed by Marsovzski (19), Shorey (8) and Findlay (2) all on singles.

levers. And, with Fontana's arrival, exceptional brakes. Year after year, this innovative manufacturer improved his products, and Jack's motorcycles benefitted from the constant progress.

The more Jack went to Italy, the more he was in demand, and the more organisers were willing to pay him well. The races were not easy for an Australian privateer rider, because there were so many Italian factories, each with their own riders. MV Agusta, Benelli, Ducati and Aermacchi were intent on victory. English-speaking riders then served as foils for the glory of their Italian opponents. The spectators cheered with joy when they saw them win. But the atmosphere was so joyful and festive that invited foreign riders shrugged off their lowly finishing places. So, at the beginning of the season, Jack finished ninth in Modena in the 500, then ninth and tenth with the 125 Honda in Riccione and Milano Maritima, and sixth in Imola in the 500. But those were just appetisers for the first Grand Prix of the season at the Nürburgring on 25 April.

If in the 500 category there are only two factory machines – the MV Agusta of Mike Hailwood and Giacomo Agostini – the competition in the 350 would be tough for the privateers. Besides these two riders and their MVs, there were the factory Hondas of Jim Redman and Bruce Beale, the Aermacchis of Gilberto Milani and Renzo Pasolini, Tarquinio Provini's Benelli, plus machines from Eastern Europe like the East German MZs, Czech Jawas and CZs, and even the Soviet Russian Vostoks.

Needless to say, British-based riders like Jack, Griff Jenkins, John Cooper or Paddy Driver on their 350 AJS or 500 Norton machinery were reduced to fighting each other to finish fifth or sixth and scrape some points. For Jack, that season on the

350 would prove frustrating, since his McIntyre AJS improved in terms of reliability but not in performance. In this category, he finished a Grand Prix race between seventh and twelfth place seven times. It was honourable, but without a single point scored, he didn't feature in the World Championship points table.

In the 500, fortunately, things went better as the McIntyre Matchless began to reveal its potential. The season started for real at the Nürburgring after the US GP in Daytona, where only Hailwood went on the MV, as the organisers refused to pay travel expenses to privateer riders. In Germany, Jack took a beautiful fourth place after a long battle with his compatriot, Jack Ahearn, and the German Walter Scheimann. The next GP was in Barcelona, where there were neither 350 nor 500 races. Yet Jack went there, finishing eighth with the 125 Honda. Eight days later, ignoring the French GP at Rouen where there were neither 350 nor 500 events, he raced in Madrid, where he must have ridden a 250 Bultaco for the first time, and finished fifth in the 125 on a similar bike.

Heading back north, he stopped in Chimay, Belgium, long enough to finish fourth in the 500 and then headed to the Tourist Trophy for a mixed bag of results. There, he finished two out of three races in tenth place, in the 250 on a DMW and in the 500 on his McIntyre G50, but he didn't finish in the 350 and, most importantly, he discovered that his beloved 500 wasn't ideal for the circuit. Nevertheless, he continued to use it until 1968. In that year, in the Senior race, for every lap he covered, he took about a minute and a half longer than Joe Dunphy, who finished second on his Beart Norton, or Mike Duff, who came in third on an Arter Matchless.

Then the 500 GPs followed suit. He took 11th in the Netherlands, 12th in Belgium, 11th in East Germany, ninth in Czechoslovakia, eighth in Monza. It was good to be in the finishing results, but those were far from the positions that earned points. Fortunately, by finishing fourth in the Ulster and fifth in Imatra, Finland, he took his total to eight points, which landed him seventh place in the world rankings.

So, by no means was Jack the best privateer in the world, and yet it was him that the organisers of the Suzuka circuit invited to go with his 350 McIntyre AJS for the Japanese Grand Prix at the end of October. He finished in seventh place there, a final twist of fate preventing him from scoring a point with this bike.

Just before flying to Japan, he had another good battle with Gyula Marsovski in Zaragoza, in which the Swiss-Hungarian privateer again emerged victorious. Business as usual, in a way.

Was it the fact that Jack found the 350 category frustrating, or did he come to the conclusion that the 350 AJS engine was no longer competitive? Whichever, upon his return from Suzuka, he decided to sell the 350 McIntyre. "That season, the 350s only raced nine times in Grands Prix. The 250s were included every time, and it was the same in International races. It was mainly this observation that pushed me to part with the AJS, and to seek out a bike on which I could return to the 250, to always be sure of being able to start twice at each meeting."

The factory game

From the inception of the motorcycle World Championships in 1949, Grand Prix racers found themselves divided into two categories: those supported by a factory, which paid them and provided them with their best bikes, and the privateers, the amateurs, who had to buy their machines and pay for their maintenance, with no hope of income other than the meagre financial rewards allocated by the organisers at the start and finish of each race.

In the 1950s, Italian factories such as Mondial, Gilera, Moto Guzzi and MV Agusta maintained official teams, most of whose riders were Italian. But there were also a few Anglo-Saxons among these privileged few. The Italian factories withdrew from competition at the end of the 1957 season, with the exception of MV Agusta, which retained only one rider.

The goal for top-level privateers was to obtain the provision of a factory machine, which benefitted from all the consistent improvements in development, and was maintained by factory mechanics.

From 1960 on, with the arrival of Honda followed by other Japanese manufacturers like Suzuki and Yamaha, it was these companies that riders sought support from. Challenging the factory machines with a customer bike, in other words, a machine that anyone could buy, was a way to get noticed and perhaps become a factory rider. As his career progressed, Jack came to symbolise this unequal struggle between factory riders and privateers. And while he had offers from factories, with bikes and dedicated mechanics, they were sporadic and not always competitive.

Phil Read with his factory Yamaha, Japanese mechanics, and a spare bike for practice.

CHAPTER 4

The World's Top Privateer

1966-1968

The following three years would be extremely successful for our hero. It was during this period that he'd earn the well-deserved nickname of the world's top privateer. That period saw his talent finally achieve its deserved results, owing to his ability to organise his racing schedule properly and prepare his bikes correctly.

One of Jack's recurring problems had been the lack of spare parts to rebuild engines after a breakdown. Having decided to abandon the 350 category in favour of returning to the 250 class, in October 1965 after returning from his last race of the year in Zaragoza, he stopped at the Bultaco factory near Barcelona to order one of the new liquid-cooled 250s. Then, after the Japanese GP, he went to England to sell the McIntyre AJS 350 to Brian Ball, via Bill Smith. With the money from that, he bought a second Matchless G50 engine, so as to no longer depend on spare parts availability in case of problems, and to improve his setup: "I had my crankshafts rebuilt in Puteaux, near Paris, in Jojo's workshop. He was a mechanical genius, an incredibly precise and meticulous guy, whose crankshafts never broke. Throughout all those years, I always kept the same engine. But I changed the cases several times, as well as the cylinder and cylinder head. A race engine is a living thing, so it must get overhauled from year to year. In the beginning, I did all my own mechanical work, but at last in the end I had two engines. They were prepared by Arthur Keeler, a mechanic who worked at the AMC factory. Every time I went to England, I went to see him to pick up a rebuilt engine and leave him the other one. He was a really precise engineer who built me fast and reliable motors."

The chassis was also improved, with Jakeman refining the fairing and Fontana providing a set of brakes, a 210mm four leading-shoe front and 210mm twin

The world's top privateer in full song at Brno in 1968.

leading-shoe rear. Over the following races, Jack fell in love with that machine. He was inexhaustible: "The McIntyre was fantastic because it was very low, smaller and lighter than the original G50. With it, I had the sensation of sitting within the bike and no longer on top of it, like with the other 500s. Since there was a lot of weight on the front, I could drift the rear wheel at will by counter-steering. It was at Spa that it really excelled. In 1968, I did a lap at an average speed of 204km/h (126mph) – no one else had ever done that with a single-cylinder bike. The top speed was about 225-230km/h (140-143mph), but I could take La Source and Eau Rouge faster than anyone else. However, when I raced in the Isle of Man with the McIntyre, it wasn't suitable for that course. It was too light, so it bounced over the bumps, especially after I set the rear suspension very hard so as to be able to drift it."

At the start of the 1966 season, he also had to learn how to prepare a two-stroke engine. "Thanks to the loan of the DMWs for the TT, I knew what to expect with this type of motor. The Bultaco 250 was a very good bike so long as you followed the factory's recommendations, and changed the parts whenever necessary. It was light and easy to ride. I quickly got the hang of it, so at the Nürburgring in April, I did several laps in front of Taveri's Honda, and finished the race just behind him. He even came over to congratulate me afterwards!"

During the 1960s, Jack worked on his bikes all alone.

However, before that at Le Mans, for Jack's first outing of the season, things hadn't gone brilliantly, either with the 250 Bultaco or with the 500 Matchless. Same thing in Imola and Milano Marittima. Racing in German-speaking territory had been more profitable, with that second place on the 250 at the Nürburgring, and especially a resounding victory in the 500 in Salzburg, coupled with a fifth place in the 250. In the 500, the competition was tough, against the factory Jawas of Stastny and Havel, fellow Australian Jack Ahearn's Norton, and Englishman Chris Conn's similar bike. At the finish, Jack was congratulated by his compatriot, and also by Mike Hailwood, who'd been watching the race and witnessed the battle. It should be noted that during these first races in Italy and then in Salzburg, Jack appeared in the rankings of the 125cc category on a Bultaco. He also finished the last GP of the season in Japan on a 125 Bultaco. Was it a machine borrowed from a friend? Or more likely loaned by the factory? A total mystery surrounds these four appearances of Jack that year in a category he did not particularly favour.

The McIntyre Matchless 500 was not at home on the TT road course, but Jack loved this race and would never miss it.

Jack with his left foot in plaster in the Spa paddock in July '67.

The first Grand Prix counting for the World Championship took place in Barcelona on 8 May, but without the 500s. Riding the 250 Bultaco, Jack finished fourth behind three factory bikes: Hailwood's Honda, Woodman's MZ and Pasolini's Aermacchi. This excellent result would reflect his entire season in the 250 category, where he would consistently prove to be the best privateer, despite there being eight or nine factory bikes on the grid each time, including the Bultacos of Ginger Molloy and Tommy Robb. Three other fourth places in Finland, the Tourist Trophy, Italy, and Japan, and a fifth place in Italy, showed his consistency in this category and especially the reliability of his machine. "Well-prepared, it was reliable. I raced at least 25 times with it, and I only broke the engine once." Jack had also equipped his Bultaco with a Jakeman fairing, slimmer than the original. With it, he won in Mettet and Chimay, both ultra-fast public-road circuits.

Jack achieved a comparable consistency in the 500 category, the most prestigious class where the Honda factory had just introduced a new four-cylinder bike to challenge the Italian MV Agusta triple. As in the 250s, Honda's riders were Hailwood and Jim Redman, facing the new Italian star, Giacomo Agostini. Privateer riders on single-cylinder bikes knew they'd have to fight among themselves to finish fourth behind those three. There were lots of privateers, all well-equipped: Kel Carruthers, John Dodds, Jack Ahearn, Chris Conn or John Cooper on Manx Nortons, Stuart Graham, Peter Williams, Ron Chandler and John Blanchard on Matchless G50s. They were all riders of Jack's calibre, all capable of beating him regularly.

The first 500 GP in Germany was a miss, with Jack finishing lower than tenth. In Holland, he came sixth, close behind Cooper and Graham. The Belgian GP turned into a nightmare: a massive storm hit the circuit just at the start. After a few laps,

Redman lost control of his Honda, crashed and broke his arm. Agostini controlled the race ahead of Hailwood. Jack was fifth among the privateers when a pheasant crossing the track hit him square in the face, breaking one lens of his goggles. Miraculously, he didn't crash, and managed to reach the pits – but fainted when he got off the bike. What bad luck – with Hailwood retiring also, he could have finished on the podium.

Jack made up for this in the following GPs: second at the Sachsenring, where he always excelled, fourth at Brno and Ulster, third in Finland and Italy. The only false note was the Tourist Trophy, where he finished eighth, out of the points.

By the end of the season – with seventh place in the 250 World Championship behind six factory riders, ahead of many other factory-supported competitors, and third in the 500 points table behind Agostini and Hailwood, the two superstars of the era – Jack had undoubtedly become one of the world's most elite road racers.

All his supporters dreamed of seeing him become a factory rider. That became a dream half-realised when he was contacted by the giant Japanese tyre company Bridgestone, which offered him the chance to ride its 50cc twin-cylinder racer in the Dutch and Japanese GPs. Jack wasn't really interested in those tiny bikes, but such

Jack riding his 250 Bultaco, a basic machine aimed at privateers in this class.

an offer can't be refused. He therefore finished eighth at Assen and sixth at the Fuji Speedway on the 50cc Bridgestone, and with this solitary point scored in Japan, he appeared for the only time in his career in the World Championship rankings in the 50cc category.

A Bridgestone advert showing Jack with his teammate, Isao Morishita.

"Riding this tiny machine didn't interest me much, but Bridgestone being such a large factory, I was lured by the possibility of getting a 350 from them. In the end this project didn't materialise, as Bridgestone eventually made an agreement with the other Japanese manufacturers to stop making bikes in order to protect their tyre sales, but I didn't regret the experience. I found out that riding these 50cc bikes was extremely difficult, because you're constantly juggling the 14-speed gearbox, and working the throttle and clutch to keep the engine at the right rpm. It's as mentally and physically exhausting as a 500, but for different reasons!"

The trip to Japan was a voyage of discovery for Jack and his Irish friend and fellow Bridgestone rider, Tommy Robb. However, adjusting to local customs wasn't easy. Wanting to take a bath, the two Westerners went to the communal bath of their inn and began soaping and scrubbing in the hot water before draining it when they left. This angered the innkeeper, as in Japan, people wash before entering the bath and stay in the clean, hot water to relax, leaving it for others to use afterwards!

Upon returning from Japan, for the first time since the start of his career Jack could spend the winter in peace without worrying about the next season. That said, hell is never far from heaven, and he would experience this harsh reality during the following season, which ought to have continued on this favourable path. But a grain of sand, or rather a piston pin, would disrupt his plans.

It was a strange experience to race the tiny twin-cylinder 50cc Bridgestone.

The 1967 season started with great news: the famous

British tuner Francis Beart contacted Jack to ask him to ride his 350 and 500 Nortons in the Isle of Man. "This offer gave me immense pleasure, because I have a clear idea of the criteria for judging my worth, and if Francis trusted me, it was a good sign," he confided to journalist Mick Woollett.

There was only one 500 GP in Germany before the Tourist Trophy, but three in the 250 championship, in Spain, France and Germany. While awaiting the GP kick-off, meetings followed one after the other all over Europe, albeit with mixed fortunes. Jack achieved honourable finishes at Modena, Pau and Milano Marittima, interspersed with some breakdowns resulting inevitably in retirement, topped by a brilliant 250/500 double at the Nürburgring – that year a non-championship event – and two podiums in Salzburg. For those men who met each other every weekend on a different race track, honours alternated with the uncertainties of racing. As they travelled from circuit to circuit, start money and cash prizes allowed them to continue earning a living from this strange activity, from a circus where so often "the clown pays with his own body to entertain people," as Mike Hailwood aptly put it.

Thus, the absence of the 500s at the Spanish GP prompted Jack to skip it and race instead at Salzburg, where his two podiums made his trip even more profitable, especially since right after that there was the German GP in nearby Hockenheim. "You had to take everything into account in organising a season," Nanou told me. "Two good start-money payments plus prize money, and 2000km less to travel, quickly improved the weekly or monthly budget."

German GP results were Jack fourth in the 250, and third in the 500 after

Hard riding at Hockenheim in 1967, with Jack in front of Mike Hailwood, Ian Burne and Billie Nelson.

fighting the whole race with Peter Williams. Jack and Nanou then left Hockenheim for Clermont-Ferrand, where the French GP awaited them. Along the way, they made a brief stop near Lyon, where Nanou's family lived.

The Charade circuit in Auvergne was one of Jack's favourites. In the race, he was battling with Rosner's 250 MZ for sixth place when he crashed. His friend Insermini asked, "Why did you have to fight against a faster bike than yours?" Jack replied, "There was a spot where I was sure I could overtake him!" Maybe not ...

Chasing Peter Williams at La Source hairpin in the 1967 Belgian GP.

The Bultaco was badly damaged, so Jack organised for it to be transported to the factory in Barcelona, where it could be repaired, then headed to the Ospedaletti street race on the coast near the French border. A fine second place in the 500 behind Bergamonti's twin-cylinder Paton paid for at least some of the Bultaco's repair bill. He had to pick up the bike quickly in Barcelona before heading to the Tourist Trophy.

Jack told me the McIntyre was not ideal at the TT. He was therefore delighted to ride Beart's Nortons, well known for being fast and reliable. But in the first practice session on the 250, the Bultaco engine suddenly seized at top speed, causing a crash

On the podium with Giacomo Agostini and John Hartle at the 1967 East German GP.

Jack at the Sachsenring in July 1967, still suffering from his broken left foot.

in which Jack damaged his hand and fractured his left foot. He was immediately operated on at Nobles Hospital, where doctors diagnosed three months of rest. Jack escaped from the hospital after nine days and returned to Paris. With his foot in a cast, he spent two weeks lying down, brooding over his bad luck. "I should have checked the engine had been reassembled properly at the factory, but I didn't have time. The engine lock up was caused by the piston pin seizing. No one had ever seen that before on a Bultaco engine, but in fact, when I disassembled it, I discovered that an incorrect-size pin had been installed."

Despite his foot injury, Jack tried to get a start in the Dutch TT at Assen, but the organisers refused to let him race. Eight days later at Spa, Jack saw a doctor who agreed to remove his cast and sign a certificate saying he could ride the bike. But he still had to walk with crutches. At the circuit, he was allowed to take part in practice and, despite his handicap, he set the fifth fastest time behind Agostini, Hailwood, Fred Stevens and Peter Williams. On the morning of the race, he asked if he could have a pusher, as allowed by the rules. This was granted him, but it would have meant he had to start last on the grid. Jack refused, insisting on starting from his rightful position. During the lunch break, Nanou worked tirelessly, negotiating with the race jury and its president, the Dutchman Henry Burik. She convinced them that Jack could start by pushing with one leg, since the start line was downhill. Positioned off to the side to avoid blocking anyone, Jack mounted his bike and, at the drop of the flag, pushed off with his only good leg, still sitting on the bike. But by the time he had enough momentum to fire up the engine, the entire field had gone. He began a furious pursuit and, despite his sore foot and difficulty braking, passed his rivals one by one, until he caught up with Williams on lap 10, then overtook

Jack and John Cooper during early morning practice at Hockenheim for the 1967 German GP.

him. Jack went on to secure fourth place in the remaining five laps behind Agostini (MV-3), Hailwood (Honda-4) and Stevens (Paton twin), after overtaking Marsovszki (Matchless) and Derek Minter (Norton) to be the first privateer and first single-cylinder home. All with a damaged left foot …

"You could almost believe that Findlay's crashes get him wound up, and make him even faster!"

The 15-day break before the East German GP was much needed for Jack to rest his foot. On the long and challenging track, he started again from last on the grid, but overtook everyone except Agostini and Matchless-mounted John Hartle to finish third. Unfortunately, eight days later in Czechoslovakia, while slipstreaming Stevens' Paton at the start of practice, a faulty bearing caused his gearbox to lock up, and Jack was thrown off. His head hit a post, his foot the ground, and he was taken to hospital in Brno with fractures to his skull, two broken vertebrae and more damage to his left foot. He remained unconscious for five days, and there were even fears for his life, but then he resumed consciousness, and pestered the doctors to let him leave hospital. Driving his truck, he headed to the Ulster GP, where after another magnificent comeback from the back of the grid, he stood on the podium behind Hailwood and Hartle. "You could almost believe that Findlay's crashes get him wound up, and make him even faster!" an English journalist wrote after this race. Indeed, Jack was tireless. After the Italian GP, where he finished ninth in the 500, using an old engine not up to par and down on top speed, he went to compete in two races in Spain with the 250 Bultaco, taking the opportunity to try out a new model lent to him by the factory.

In the end, despite all these setbacks, and the races missed due to falls for which he was not responsible, Jack was 14th in the 250 and fifth in the 500 in the final standings.

Jack with the Cardani 500 in April 1968.

The Cardani frame was made according to Jack's instructions by Belletti in Milan.

Right: Dan Shorey, Rex Butcher and Barry Smith try to persuade a reluctant Cardani to start in Imola, though the watching Tommy Robb and Ginger Molloy seem doubtful.

Left: Jack talking with Daniele Fontana in their Milan workshop.

During the 1967-68 off season, at the instigation of Daniele Fontana, Jack decided to leave Paris for Milan to settle near his friend, and strengthen their collaboration even further. For over a year, Fontana had been working with a partner on a major new project: the construction of a 500cc three-cylinder Grand Prix machine. The initial engine drawings were made in 1966, but the demand for brakes was such that Fontana fell behind in its completion. In his mind, there was no doubt that Jack should not only be the rider of the bike, but should also be involved in its construction. Jack and Nanou moved into an apartment in Milan, very close to Fontana's place. His factory was in an old farmhouse: a large room housed the brake production line, while Jack had his own workshop next door, including a test bench. Around the grounds, there were chickens and rabbits, and a vegetable garden, as Fontana wanted to keep his rural roots. "I also loved to go trout fishing because there's no shortage of streams north of Milan, but my work hardly left me any free time for that. During that time, we were producing 600 to 700 brakes per year, of various sizes, all handmade. It was a lot of work."

The Cardani project had been launched in 1966, with Carlo Savare, a brewing industrialist, providing the funding. Fontana counted on Jack to participate in the chassis design. Indeed, this frame would be directly inspired by the McIntyre chassis, using identical geometry. "The only difference," Jack explained, "is that we didn't keep the bottom tube bypassing the engine, but made a classic double cradle whose lower tubes pass under the engine."

This machine aroused high hopes, and fans dreamed of seeing it challenge Agostini's MV Agusta. But then a bolt from the blue struck the Grand Prix world, even before the 1968 season began: the Honda factory announced its immediate withdrawal from competition. Suzuki followed suit, leaving only Yamaha to continue running its 125 and 250 four-cylinder bikes. European factories and privateers alike saw it as an opportunity for better results, but the withdrawal also meant the hope of obtaining a factory ride was ended for many. But Jack didn't care, and carefully

In 1968, Jack is riding Francis Beart's immaculate 250 Aermacchi in the Lightweight TT.

A riders' meeting at the Sachsenring in 1968 to form a union. From left to right: Lewis Young, Billie Nelson, Kel Carruthers, Fred Stevens, Dan Shorey, John Hartle, Jack, John Cooper and Rex Butcher. Nanou and Pat Nelson listen at the back.

Early laps of the 1968 Belgian GP in Spa: Alberto Pagani on his Linto leads Giacomo Agostini and Kel Carruthers, with Jack tucked away behind the bubble, .

A hard battle between the 350 Aermacchis of Jack and local star Brian Steenson in the 1968 Ulster GP.

planned his 1968 season. The Cardani project's future was uncertain, so he prepared his Matchless as meticulously as usual, and likewise his 250 Bultaco. Good news came from England, where Francis Beart offered him the chance to ride his 250 and 350 Aermacchis at the Tourist Trophy, having ended his longtime focus on Manx Nortons in favour of the lightweight Italian bikes. That was a substantial advantage for Jack, who did not have to use his own machines for these long races and wear them out.

At the start of the season, Jack warmed up in Alicante, finishing fifth in the 250 and 500 with his usual bikes. But all the attention of the tifosi and the press was focused on the Cardani: when would it make its debut? The meetings at Rimini and Cesenatico came and went, but no Cardani. It did a few test laps at Imola, but Jack raced with the Matchless there and finished ninth. It was clear he was distracted. That impression was confirmed at the first GP at the Nürburgring, where he finished fifth in the 250, but retired due to clutch failure in the 500. Was the Cardani project affecting the preparation of the McIntyre Matchless?

Much later, Jack would say how much this project drained his energy: "Throughout the winter, Daniele and I worked 12 hours a day, seven days a week. The engine ran for the first time at the end of February 1968; the next day, we took the bike to Monza. But that winter was icy, so I could only ride 100km before stopping. We made two more attempts, but fog and frost stopped us. As the season approached, I understood more and more that the Cardani wouldn't be ready. I was

A typical road racing scene running between houses at the 1968 Czech GP at Brno: Jack leading Carruthers, Hartle, Shorey, Nelson, Williams and the pack.

Two Nortons and a Matchless entering the Queckenberg hairpin at the Sachsenring in 1968. Kel Carruthers leads Jack and John Cooper.

exhausted, and I had neglected preparing my Matchless engines. So, I decided to rely again on the McIntyre."

For the second Grand Prix in Barcelona, the Cardani was there. Jack went for the first practice session, completed a lap and stopped, suspecting a strange noise in the engine. He started the race with the Matchless, and began an impressive streak of second places on the single behind Agostini and his invincible MV triple.

Three podiums at meetings in Germany and the Netherlands in the lead-up to the Tourist Trophy didn't erase the disappointment that awaited Jack there in the

The start of the 1968 Czech GP in Brno: 30 bikes, but just one factory entry – Agostini's MV Agusta carrying No 1.

Isle of Man, with retirement in the 250 and 500, and a sixth place finish in the 350 Junior TT on the Beart Aermacchi, after an exhausting race due to overly soft rear suspension.

There's a nice anecdote about Jack's TT visit that year. Francis Beart, meticulous as always, had his rev counters checked for accuracy. He suggested Jack have the McIntyre G50's checked too, which revealed it displayed 500rpm higher than the correct speed. "Just doing this check immediately gave me more power, since now I could rev my engine that much harder," said Jack. Strange, but true ...

Francis Beart was happy with the Junior TT result, and invited Jack to race his 350 Aermacchi in the Dutch TT at Assen. Jack was delighted at the idea of doing three races there, but the organisers refused the last-minute entry. After finishing tenth in the 250 race, Jack showed them what he was capable of by staying several laps

Jack riding his Bultaco in the Isle of Man Lightweight TT.

in the lead ahead of Agostini in the 500, finishing in a good second place after a fierce battle with John Cooper and Peter Williams.

Daniele Fontana joined Jack in Holland with the Cardani. The two men hoped to be able to carry out tests at Zandvoort before the Belgian GP at Spa the following weekend, but in the end it was at Zolder that the Cardani completed a few laps. "For the first time the Cardani was running properly," he confided to the English press. "It's as good-handling as the McIntyre G50, but the engine has more power and torque. Zolder is a short circuit, so I only used five of the seven gears."

Despite this conclusive test, Fontana felt the bike was not ready to take part in the fast, engine-killing Belgian GP. Having doubts about the reliability of the valve springs, he took it back to Italy, to concentrate on being ready for the Italian GP in the September.

Who would be able to challenge Jack at Spa riding a single-cylinder bike like he did? On the first weekend of July 1968, he flew through the big curves of the Belgian circuit, completing a lap at an average speed of over 204km/h (127mph), and was the only one to finish the 15 laps without being lapped by Agostini on the MV Agusta triple. That was followed by a third place in East Germany, behind Agostini and Pagani's prototype Linto twin, and two second places in Czechoslovakia and Finland. It took carburettor problems to restrict him to fifth place in Ulster, where he also raced in the 350 on a borrowed Aermacchi, finishing out of the points.

Those brilliant results did not mask a harsh reality: the riders had had enough of the attitude of the organisers. In the Sachsenring, a meeting had been held under the Findlay awning, attended by the 12 best privateers of the day in the larger-capacity classes. At the end of their discussion, they decided to create the Grand Prix Riders' Association. Nanou was unanimously appointed secretary-general, recognising that she had always been there to help the riders and negotiate with organisers, so her authority and capability were well established. In announcing this in *Motor Cycle News*, John Brown quoted Jack: "We are professionals, and we deserve more respect from the organisers. The term privateer is not accurate. We are professionals in a form of show business. It's a business like any other, and the fact that we do it because of our passion for the sport has been used for too long to take advantage of us."

At the end of the year, Jack presented his plan to improve the Grands Prix in *Motor Cycle* and *Motor Cycle News*. But columnist John Brown expressed doubts when the riders said, "If the organisers don't accept our conditions, we will not go racing." There were enough riders to fill the grid, with enough ready to ride with things as they were.

But let's get back to Jack's third place in East Germany. It didn't come about by chance, for at the start of the year a new Italian machine had appeared: the twin-cylinder Linto 500. Conceived by Umberto Premoli, its engine consisted of two 250 Aermacchi cylinders paired on the same crankcase. The development had taken some time to complete because, while immediately more powerful than the singles, the new engine proved fragile. But from the summer of 1968, the Linto continued to progress in the hands of its rider, Alberto Pagani, giving Jack serious food for thought. In fact, he was asking himself the same questions of the 250 category, thinking that his single-cylinder Bultaco had now been overtaken by the twin-cylinder Yamaha. During August, Jack bought such a bike, which he used to finish fifth in the Italian GP where, in the 500, he had to retire in a race dominated by Italian machines MV Agusta, Benelli, Linto and Paton.

Despite the love he had for his Matchless, and a victory on it in Austria, Jack began wondering about his future in the 500. He felt that the Cardani was a dead end: Daniele Fontana was overwhelmed by the demand for his brakes and had insufficient time to spend on developing the motorcycle. Just then, he was contacted by the Linto management, who offered him the chance to try their bike in mid-October at Monza. It was a test session that ended up with him crashing flat out at 240km/h (150 mph) in the middle of a straight when the gearbox locked up because of a broken primary drive pinion. For Jack, it was a racing hazard like any other, especially since Premoli said the reason for the failure had been identified: faulty heat-treating of the gear pinion.

The important thing was that Jack had been able to experience the potential of the Linto and to appreciate that it would easily get the better of the single-cylinder bikes. Premoli announced the production of a small series of 12 machines intended for privateer riders, and the factory's intention to race two works bikes the following year, entrusted to Alberto Pagani, who had just completed a debut season aboard the factory prototype, and a second rider. They did not hide the fact that they would like that rider to be Jack.

The Australian did not hesitate: he understood the Cardani was a dead end and that his single-cylinder McIntyre G50 would no longer be competitive. The day after his last outing on the bike at Vallelunga, near Rome, where he twice finished sixth, still bruised by his fall, he placed an ad in the British newspapers to sell his beautiful McIntyre Matchless. At that time, he was the best known rider in the 500 Grands Prix after Agostini, and duly recognised as the best privateer in the world, admired for his results, straightforward personality and affable nature. Eleventh in the world in 250, vice world champion in 500, Jack was on top of the world.

Jack challenging Frantisek Srnà on his CZ twin.

Grand Prix or Local Meeting

Grands Prix, small International races, or prestigious National races on British circuits? All riders had to make such choices when planning their calendar at the beginning of the season. That was followed by a large number of letters to various organisers to secure a start and negotiate travel expenses. Grand Prix races had prestige, and above all, earning points and places in the World Championship points table enhanced a rider's résumé. But paradoxically, some Grand Prix races were less competitive than certain smaller races, as evidenced by the time differences between finishers. And the distance to travel to these races discouraged riders who couldn't make it pay, to such an extent that some top-level riders raced only in Britain, where they felt at home, and where races were certain to always be hard-fought.

Hugh Anderson and his factory Suzuki mechanics.

"The time gaps at the finish of a Grand Prix can be deceiving," Rex Butcher, a British rider who raced with Jack in 1967 and 1968, told me. "In fact, the level was very high, and the riders were very close to each other – 20 guys could beat you and each other every Sunday. But the long straights in Grand Prix circuits skewed the game, because slipstreaming played a major role. If at the beginning of the race a group of riders took advantage of that, they'd leave everyone else behind, and once you were detached and riding alone, your chance to catch a group or even a pair of riders ahead of you had gone. I remember doing that once with Kel Carruthers at Monza – we kept drafting past each other, and left everyone else behind. On short circuits, it was different – there weren't enough straights to do that, and so consequently you'd get many packs of riders all together. It was pretty hectic!"

A parade of all the day's race winners at Albi in 1963: (from left) Hans-Georg Anscheidt (50cc), Ulf Svensson (125cc) and Jack Findlay (250cc).

CHAPTER 5

From Glory to Disaster

1969-1970

1969 began with a milestone for Jack: he officially became the second rider for the Linto factory team, alongside Albert Pagani. At the same time, he struck a deal with Jérôme Laperrousaz, a young French filmmaker who planned to shoot a movie about Grand Prix racing, focusing on him, the Australian vice world champion on his personal bike, bravely facing the invincible Giacomo Agostini and his MV Agusta. The filming was scheduled to start at the Tourist Trophy in June.

"For the first time in my life, I'll be racing in the 500 on a bike that I didn't pay for out of my own pocket," Jack aptly remarked when announcing his signing with Linto. With Pagani officially a development rider, it could be inferred that Linto was counting on Jack to be its top rider.

In the excitement of this contract, Jack's fans considered him finally a factory rider. In reality, Linto was a typical industrial venture beloved of Italian entrepreneurs of the time. The designer, Lino Tonti, was an engineer who worked at Mondial and Moto Guzzi. The financier, Umberto Premoli, a major car dealer, was a racing enthusiast who had some competition experience himself. The Linto engine used standard OHV Aermacchi 250cc racing components, namely cylinders, cylinder heads, and pushrod valve gear, assembled in a bottom end designed by Tonti, with dedicated crankcases, crankshaft and six-speed gearbox. Two prototype Lintos had been built in 1968, and a small series of about 15 machines were built for the 1969 season, with three for the works riders, which would be blue, while the others, painted red, would be sold to

> *"For the first time in my life, I'll be racing in the 500 on a bike that I didn't pay for out of my own pocket,"*

Jack riding the Linto 500 in the first GP of the 1969 season, the Spanish round in Jarama.

private customers. The location of the machines' assembly was not truly a factory, but more like a large workshop similar to those of the rival Paton team on the other side of Milan. But, in Italy, passion makes miracles happen.

Staying true to his habits, Jack decided to race in a second category. He still had his 250 Yamaha, but it was an older model. The Yamaha factory had just released two new customer race bikes, the 250 TD2, which succeeded the TD1C, and the 350 TR2, a rocket ship that immediately attracted widespread attention in the Daytona 200-miler, where it almost beat Cal Rayborn's victorious 750cc Harley-Davidson. Acquiring one of the new 350 TR2s was complicated. Daniele Fontana was in contact with an American named Dan Hunt who wanted to import his brakes to the US. Hunt could get one of the brand-new TR2 engines, but a frame needed to be built for him. After the Cardani, that would be the second frame designed by Jack and Daniele, still inspired by the McIntyre, with the help of specialist frame-maker Belletti in Milan, which the previous year wrapped tubing around a factory Honda RC181 four-cylinder 500 engine for Mike Hailwood.

Jack's first outings aboard the 500 Linto were disastrous. In Rimini, Modena and Le Mans, he suffered repeated breakdowns. It was all the more frustrating as Keith Turner won at Le Mans on a Linto and, 15 days later, Maurice Hawthorne took his to victory in Bourg-en-Bresse. At Le Mans, Jack debuted his 'American' 350 Yamaha, but also suffered a breakdown on that. It was the same scenario at Imola, with two retirements. A 14th place in the 350 and a seventh place in the 500 at Cesenatico brought an end to that series of disasters, but there was nothing to boast about. The first Grands Prix were approaching, and the two bikes were not ready. Jack didn't go to Mettet, where he was entered, to prepare for the Spanish GP, held for the first time at the Jarama circuit, north of Madrid. Being short of training, Jack was not comfortable. Yet, he still managed to finish fifth in the 350, but his 500 engine wasn't running smoothly and eventually broke. He rushed to Italy, where Premoli's team managed to rebuild an engine for him with spare parts en route to Hockenheim and the German GP. Doing well in the 350, where he momentarily held third place, Jack was overtaken right at the end by Stastny and his Jawa. It was a good omen for the 500 race, where he quickly settled into second position behind Agostini. But, as in the 350, an old hand came to give him trouble, with German Karl Hoppe on the URS four-cylinder getting the better of him after a few laps spent battling together, delighting his local fans. Still, it was a first podium for the Findlay/Linto duo, so there was light at the end of the tunnel for the vice-world champion.

Jack had to work on repairing and preparing his Linto himself.

At Le Mans for the next GP, Jérôme Laperrousaz's film crew was there to start shooting the rest of the races that Jack would be in throughout the summer. Having been delayed at the start on the 350, Jack finished far off the leaders, while in the 500, his engine misfired straight out of the pits. After two laps, he was forced to retire. Hoping to repair the motor with parts sourced locally, he headed to the NW200 in Northern Ireland. It was a long journey for yet another fiasco with the Linto, but a decent third place in the 350 was a consolation prize.

From Italy, parts were sent to the Isle of Man, where he met up with Aermacchi engine specialist Syd Lawton, a passionate sponsor and friend of Francis Beart, who lent him a well-prepared 350 Aermacchi and, just in case, also brought a 383cc version capable of racing in the 500 class. When Jack and Syd dismantled the Linto

Jack's solitary satisfactory race with the Linto in 1969 was the West German GP in Hockenheim, battling with Karl Hoppe's URS four for second place.

engine, they discovered everything was wrong inside. They tried to fix it, but during the first TT practice session it broke again, with serious damage. Jack was competing in three races that week: in the 250 on the Yamaha he had to retire, and in the 500 on the borrowed jumbo-Aermacchi. But he took Lawton's 350 bike to a respectable third place, much to the satisfaction of Syd, who was the importer for those machines in England, as well as for Fontana brakes!

Back on the Continent, Jack learned he wouldn't have a Linto available for the Dutch GP. In Italy, Premoli hadn't hidden his dissatisfaction with seeing his top rider break so many engines, and he admitted his team was sorely lacking in spare parts and money. Because several of the privateer Lintos had also given trouble, to appease their customers' discontent, they'd been provided with enough spare parts to repair them more or less free of charge. Suffice to say, there was a fleet of very unhappy Linto users, as much out of luck as their figurehead wearing the blue kangaroo helmet.

At the cost of three sleepless nights, Syd Lawton got his 385 Aermacchi ready for the Dutch TT at Assen, a circuit where the very manoeuvrable bike should have been competitive in the 500 category. After a very good start, and spending two laps ahead of Agostini, which delighted the crowd, Jack found himself in fourth place, followed by his Italian friend Gilberto Milani, also on an Aermacchi. Two laps before the finish, Milani managed to pass Jack, but with only a few hundred metres to go, the Italian's engine broke. He continued freewheeling, inevitably slowing down as he did so, which should have allowed his opponent to overtake. But, being a truly great sportsman, Jack didn't do so, and finished the race behind Milani, in fifth place

The Jada frame built to house the 350 Yamaha motor was directly inspired by the McIntyre G50.

Jack and Nanou before a practice session at Le Mans with the 350 Yamaha.

(thus achieving a double, since he was also fifth in the 350 race). In the parc fermé, he explained his gesture with his usual straightforwardness: "Gilberto passed me because he was better than me. I couldn't deprive him of his place 50 metres from the finish just because his engine blew up."

With the film team led by Jérôme Laperrousaz, the 'Findlay Clan' was a regular part of the paddock. The other riders were pleased with this exposure, because the director and the cameramen were also interested in them, and filmed them a lot.

Jack riding Francis Beart's 350 Aermacchi to sixth place in the 1969 Junior TT.

At Assen, Jack learned his Linto engines would not be ready for the next GP in Spa – a track so fast that it was useless to bring out the jumbo-Aermacchi for the 500 race again. Generously, Peter Williams, who had raced in Assen and finished second, offered to lend Jack his spare 500 Arter Matchless, provided that Tom Arter, his sponsor, agreed. The latter said yes without hesitation as soon as Peter called him, so Jack would ride that bike in Spa in front of the movie cameras.

Qualifying on the front row in practice, Jack immediately tucked in behind the second-placed Pagani's Linto, which was much faster than his Matchless, but after five laps he went missing, no longer going past the pits. Nanou panicked, as on a fast circuit surrounded by guardrails like Spa, crashing was especially hazardous. After the race it turned out that Jack had fallen at one of the fastest parts of the circuit, the Masta kink, a flat-out sequence of two bends taken at over 220km/h (137mph), just after overtaking Pagani. Apart from a scratch on his face, Jack was completely unharmed, but the bike was totally wrecked. He said later that during the high-speed flick from side to side, he had the impression that the fork locked, which might have caused his fall. But French rider André-Luc Appietto, who had been overtaken by Findlay during practice on his 500 Paton twin, had another explanation: "When a rider on a slower

A backup ride for the 1969 TT, the over-bored 380 Aermacchi Jack rode in the Senior race.

Scratching hard on the 350 Yamaha at Assen.

bike manages to overtake someone on a faster one somewhere like that, and at that speed, he is really over and beyond the limits of his bike."

As soon as the race was over and the wrecked Matchless had been returned to the paddock, it was all hands on deck. The next weekend they were racing in East Germany, so there was not a minute to be lost. Fortunately, the film crew was there to help. One of its cars would rush to Italy to retrieve a Linto engine and take it to the Sachsenring, while Jack took the Matchless back to Calais to put it on a boat for England, where Tom Arter would collect

Jérôme Laperrousaz directing his film crew in the Belgian GP paddock.

Taken by an anonymous spectator and published by Motor Cycle magazine, Jack's spectacular Spa crash right in front of Pagani's front wheel.

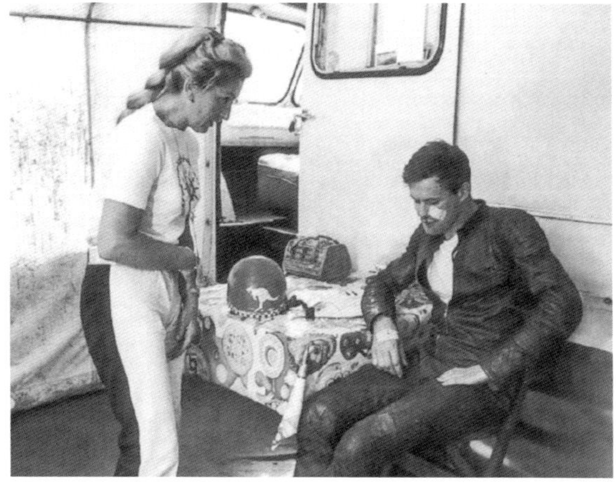

A scene from the movie Continental Circus: Nanou helps Jack after his crash at the 500 Belgian GP race.

it. Jack would have to pay him for the damage. The fee budgeted for Jack in the film's finances would cover that cost. "Jack received 50,000 francs from us for the film, which corresponded to about ten to 12 start money bonuses, so it wasn't a negligible part of his budget for that season," explained Laperrousaz later.

However, the film would not be released until the spring of 1972. Filming continued until the end of the 1969 season, with cameras cruelly recording every movement of Jack and Nanou, caught in a storm beyond their control. Jack's bad luck continued for race after race. At the Sachsenring, the entire paddock was stunned by the tragic death of the diminutive Bill Ivy, the 1967 125cc world champion, who that season had agreed to ride the new V4 Jawa 350, on which he had twice led Agostini's MV in races. 'Little Bill' was killed during Saturday morning practice due to an engine seizure on his Jawa. The weather was gloomy that weekend, the track wet from the first races on Sunday morning. On his 350 Yamaha and the 500 Linto, Jack had two more retirements to his name. Just as he was leaving the Sachsenring, the head of the Jawa team approached him with an offer to ride the 350 the following week in the Czechoslovakian GP at Brno. Jack said yes.

But he was caught in the eye of the storm: 'Findlay's Jinx', headlined an English newspaper. Jinx, bad luck, the evil eye, worse – the curse. In the first practice session, the 350 Jawa seized its two-stroke engine and threw Jack to the ground. Broken collarbone. And always the relentless eye of Laperrousaz's camera, which unknowingly now gave the leading role to Nanou, the tireless companion who cared for, supported, cheered up and encouraged him to keep moving forward.

Only 15 days later, despite his injury, our hero was at the start of the Finnish GP. Driving his truck with one hand to get there, it was Nanou who changed gears! At Imatra, he finished seventh in the 350, a great feat, but broke down yet again in the 500 with the Linto. The film *Continental Circus* would magnificently capture the grit and courage of this man who never gave up. From Finland, he headed to Northern Ireland, where he believed he could repair his Linto before the race. His hopes were dashed from the very first laps of practice: the engine was unusable. The time spent on the Linto took his attention away from the Yamaha, resulting in another retirement in the 350 race.

However, Jack did not spend a minute questioning himself. The Jawa factory offered to join them for a small race in Jicìn , Czechoslovakia, to familiarise himself with its 350, which he could ride again for the Italian and Yugoslavian GPs. Despite retiring from the race during this trial run, he told Mick Woollett: "I was quite reserved about this bike to start with, but the more I rode it, the more I liked it. At Jicìn , the track was wet in practice, but I covered nearly 160km – it handles well,

Jack pushes the 350 Jawa V4 into life in Brno.

The Bedford sliding door truck: a movie star as well as Jack and Nanou's home and transport.

accelerates like a bullet, and has a good gearbox."

In a phone call, Premoli announced some good news: a new Linto engine would be waiting for him at Imola. Except Jack wouldn't get to enjoy it: the practice sessions were satisfactory, but in the race, unfortunately, the 350 Jawa acted up from the start, and a violent seizure finally threw him off. The season was over for Jack, who would have to endure the final humiliation of seeing Alberto Pagani win the Italian GP on his Linto and, a little later, Silvio Grassetti triumph at the Yugoslavian GP with the 350 Jawa.

Riding the V4 Jawa in the 350 Italian GP, which didn't end well.

Jack and Nanou retreated to their apartment in Milan, the Laperrousaz team returned home, and the best privateer in the world had just experienced the most disastrous season of his career, both in terms of results and finances. His sixth place in the 350 championship and 13th in the 500 did not reflect his true value, nor the ordeals he had endured throughout the season. And again, everything had to be made over in preparation for the following season. For as soon as the disastrous season ended, Jack did not complain about his fate, but thought only about the next one.

But what to do? Even if a Linto was still available, he could no longer trust this bike. Abandon the 500s in favour of the 250s and 350s? Unthinkable. The 500 was the premier category, where he had been World Championship runner-up just two years earlier, and where he could best showcase his talents and earn the best start money. But with what bike to start over again? For a brief moment, there were rumours that MV Agusta was considering hiring a second rider to support Agostini, and that Findlay would be a good choice. Just as briefly, another rumour suggested the potential favourite for this choice was Kel Carruthers. In fact, nothing came of it and, at the end of 1970, MV hired another Italian, Paton rider Angelo Bergamonti. With no serious offers, Jack eventually opted for a 500 Seeley frame with a Matchless engine.

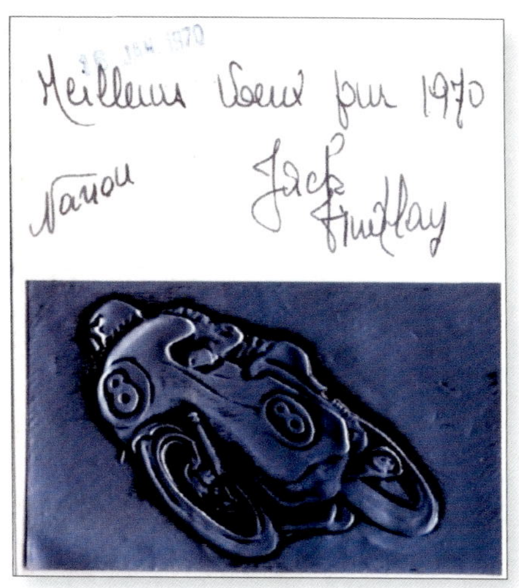

A greeting card from our heroes.

Jack rode a 350 Yamaha twin in the 1970 Daytona 200 race.

In 1970, Jack started the GP season with a Seeley-framed Matchless 500.

Colin Seeley, the former sidecar champion who had become a constructor, had bought the entire Matchless racing project, improving the G50 engine to install it in a frame of his own design, adaptable to 350 and 500 versions. His bikes had achieved great success in Britain so, like his friend Tommy Robb, without much enthusiasm, Jack ordered a 500 Seeley, hoping to regain his ranking on the world stage.

In January, for the first time, he was invited to two races in South Africa, in

Pietermaritzburg and Kyalami. He took his special 350 TR2 there, but the trip ended with two retirements. Barely back home again in Milan, he flew out to Daytona, where Dan Hunt had entered him in two races: the 100-Miler on a 250 where he finished 23rd, and the 200-Mile race on a new 350 Yamaha, fitted with a Fontana front brake, which didn't make it to the finish line. At the Speedway, he saw the new 500 Kawasaki H1Rs in action, and immediately understood that those coming to Europe would pose a new threat in Grand Prix racing. But, like the 500 Suzuki XR45, which also raced at Daytona, where it was clocked at 234km/h (145 mph), they were only available through an importer, which alone decided which rider should be entrusted with each bike. Even though the new Kawasakis didn't show great reliability in the Daytona 200, a long and gruelling race, they underlined that two-stroke engines were taking over in the premier class.

Jack's first outing with his brand-new Seeley G50 in Europe took place at Le Mans, where his second place in the 350 and fifth in the 500 won the combined overall classification of the two races. However, his subsequent events were disappointing, peppered with retirements and lowly finishes. The Kawasaki threat was becoming clearer, with a good half-dozen of them in regular action, and the customer Lintos of Ellis, Marsovszki, Dodds and Turner increasingly reliable and capable of good finishes. Even with two identical Seeleys to his on the podium of the German GP behind Agostini, Jack quickly understood the limits of this motorcycle. Up until the Tourist Trophy in early June, he enjoyed only disappointment, and his fourth places at the Yugoslavian GP and then in the Senior TT did not console him. The Seeley Matchless was no longer competitive; something else had to be found to keep him in contention.

With the help of Dan Hunt, Jack tried to find a factory Suzuki TR500 engine in the US, but he could only come up with spare parts. However, he managed to obtain the factory specs to improve the cylinders, and to make exhaust pipes. So, with the help of Suzuki tuner and dealer Kurt Weber in Switzerland, Jack acquired a 500 Suzuki Cobra road engine, and worked tirelessly to extract the necessary power from it. By the end of June at the Dutch TT, the engine was squeezed into the Seeley frame, but nothing worked properly. However, a few days later, at Spa, the bike showed great speed – but it still had its original clutch and road gearbox.

Despite retiring with holed pistons, Jack felt he made the right choice, and that he was going in

Installing a Suzuki Cobra 500 engine in the Seeley frame proved a good bet.

Riding the Seeley-framed Suzuki 500 in East Germany.

the right direction. But in race after race with this 500, the right setup proved elusive, and retirements accumulated. A glimmer of hope arose after the Finnish GP, in a race held on the Keimola circuit near Helsinki, where he finished fifth in each race. The resurrection of his hopes was confirmed right afterwards in Ulster, with a beautiful fourth place behind Agostini, Peter Williams on a light, fast Arter Matchless, and Percy Tait's Triumph twin. The 500 Suzuki engine started to work well. That day, only five riders had lapped at over 160km/h (100 mph), the first four and the Frenchman Christian Ravel, who'd been very fast on a 500 Kawasaki H1R before crashing.

A victory for Jack on the 350 in a race in Tampere, Finland, restored some morale, but the Grand Prix season ended in double frustration in Barcelona, particularly with the 350, which broke down on the last lap after Jack had fought hard to reach sixth place.

At the end of October, there was a meeting inaugurating the brand-new Paul Ricard Circuit, near Marseille. Jack was listed as finishing 16th, but in fact he stopped a few laps before the end. But like all the other riders, he was pleased to discover an organiser who listened to them, and a circuit which met all their concerns, with a wide track with good run-off areas in the turns, and a large asphalt paddock with numerous clean and comfortable sanitary facilities. For everyone, the circuit showed what a Grand

The last 1970 GP, in Spain, showed the potential of the Seeley-framed Suzuki.

Prix venue could and should be, where riders were treated with dignity. Safety on the track, comfort off it, that was the example to follow, and exactly what the GPRA riders had been demanding at their general assembly two years earlier, and which Jack had clearly stated in the English press.

But it would take time for those things to fall into place, for circuits to be designed from the outset to ensure good safety, and to replace the dangerous public road circuits.

But still the circus continued, and there was a new season to prepare for ...

Hazards and danger

Jérôme Laperrousaz was criticised for the shocking start to his film, which shows a succession of crashes, each more terrible than the one before. But this dramatization of motorcycle road racing was very real. Circuits used between the 1950s and the 1970s were horribly dangerous, with one or more riders dying almost every Sunday, given the large number of races across Europe. The vast majority of them were little known, and it took the repeated disappearance of celebrated champions for the riders' safety demands to be met. No one was safe from sustaining a fatal accident on these improvised tracks, which wound between walls, trees and houses.

The dangerous Yugoslav track in Opatija where riders were speeding between the rock cliff and the sea.

World champions like Keith Campbell, Tom Phillis, Werner Haas, Bill Ivy, and the iconic Jarno Saarinen and Renzo Pasolini paid for their passion with their lives. At the top of the macabre hierarchy of accursed tracks was, of course, the Isle of Man Tourist Trophy, but even on less dangerous circuits, serious accidents occurred. It took a long time for the last natural circuits to disappear at the end of the 1980s and for the technical regulations and track arrangements to eventually limit fatal crashes as much as possible. But accidents in the 2000s have shown that even with all possible precautions, motorcycle sport will always remain a high-risk activity.

CHAPTER 6

Return to the Top

1971-1972

As soon as he began using the Suzuki engine in the Seeley frame, in the middle of the 1970 season, Jack understood its potential. But there was still a lot of work to do to raise it a notch. Jack had his ideas about what a good frame should be, and he needed a forwards weight distribution similar to that of the McIntyre. The Seeley was too long, and had more weight on the rear. But why complicate life? Upon examination, it appeared that the T500 Suzuki motor was barely larger than the TR3 Yamaha engine, housed in the chassis Jack and Daniele built for the 1969 season. The best solution was indeed to mount this motor into that frame and to race in the 350 class with a standard TR3, since Jack considered this category secondary.

Adapting the McIntyre-type frame to equip it with the 500cc Suzuki engine was possible. Its dimensions were close to those of the TR350 Yamaha – it was a bit longer by about 5cm, and a bit higher too, but luckily, it did fit into the frame, even if the fins of the cylinder head did lightly scrape the upper tubes, which did not make assembly or disassembly easy. Of course, the mounting points had to be modified, but the swingarm remained the same. A new, larger-capacity fuel tank was installed, along with a new fork made by Swiss chassis constructor Marly Drixl, whose lower sliders were machined to ensure better heat dissipation. Throughout the history of the Jada-Suzuki, Jack found people to help him in Switzerland.

Jack would later say that the Jada was the realisation of one of his dreams: a motorcycle entirely designed and built by himself and Daniele – hence the JaDa name. Like the McIntyre in its time, the bike turned out to be one of the lightest in its category, proof that his ideas on chassis design were sound.

In March, Jack again flew to Daytona, where Dan Hunt had prepared a three-

Jack working in his Milan workshop, bench-testing a Suzuki 500 engine.

cylinder 500 Kawasaki H1R for him. While Jack had time to gauge its potential during qualifying, he mainly noticed its fragility in the race, with a broken crankshaft after just three laps. Returning to Europe with this Kawasaki, he conducted further tests before deciding to race with his Jada-Suzuki, which he took to Germany for its first outing at the Nürburgring. It was a good gauge to compare it with its rivals. Starting from seventh position, in the second row, Jack finished fourth. He was

Jack and his sponsor, Dan Hunt, in Daytona.

satisfied with his new mount. Retirements in the Austrian, German and Dutch GPs did not discourage him. The Jada had potential; its engine held well in short races (he finished third at Ziesdorf in Austria, then fourth in Tubbergen in Holland) but needed to gain added reliability in the much longer GP races.

At the Belgian GP on the Spa circuit, Jack's favourite, he qualified the Jada on the front row. Besides Agostini's MV, there were only two-stroke motorcycles at the front of the field: the Husqvarna of Sweden's Bo Granath – a handmade one-off special like the Jada – and the Kawasakis of French riders Christian Ravel, Eric Offenstadt and Briton Dave Simmonds.

In the race, Agostini naturally took the lead, but second place was hotly contested between Ravel, Offenstadt, and Jack. The latter two had an advantage, as they knew their bikes had the necessary range to finish the race non-stop while, in theory at least, Ravel would need to refuel. In fact, the young Frenchman deliberately ignored signals to stop, choosing to keep going and risk running out of fuel, with second place at stake. Tragically, this gamble proved fatal, as he crashed on the last lap in one of the fastest corners on the circuit, when his bike ran out of fuel and seized. Hitting the newly installed metal guardrails at very high speed, he was killed instantly. His motorcycle almost hit Jack, who finished third behind Offenstadt.

At the finish, Jack was furious at these two riders, teammates no less, who raced at such a frenzied pace, making him take unnecessary risks, since Agostini was so far ahead, and the fifth-placed rider well behind them. For Jack, nobody should risk their life on a gamble like that – you don't race without good judgement. Veterans of the Continental Circus like him would have done what Insermini recounted: ten

The H1R Kawasaki 500 (no.70) that Jack rode in Daytona was neither fast nor reliable.

'sensible' laps, then a sprint to the finish over the last two or three. It might not have changed the final tragedy, except that, throughout the race, Jack had feared one of his rivals might crash and take him down as well – as so nearly happened.

It was this race which probably highlighted the gap between the new generation of riders arriving in the '70s and the seasoned veterans of the circuit, of which Jack was becoming an emblematic figure. These 'old-timers' continued to believe that it was the rider's responsibility to ensure their own safety by taking into account the dangers of a circuit, grumbling that "a tree never crossed a road," and they were concerned about circuits offering "too much safety" because the same daring young riders could take risks there without fearing serious injury.

In any case, from this Belgian Grand Prix onwards, the Jada with its Suzuki engine was at its peak and capable of giving its best. It was reliable: Jack finished several International races and two GPs well-placed, before arriving in Northern Ireland for the Ulster GP, where the weather was gloomy. From the start of practice Jack proved to be the fastest man on the circuit, which was almost a mini Tourist Trophy course, winding through fields with a similar landscape lined by trees, poles and various obstacles. With Agostini and his MV absent (having already won the world title three races early), the Jada faced the two factory-engined Suzukis of Kiwi Keith Turner and Dutchman Rob Bron. But they couldn't keep up with Jack, who broke away to score his first Grand Prix victory on a bike he'd built with his own hands, with a modified street motor he patiently developed himself. It was also Suzuki's first ever GP victory in the blue riband 500cc category.

Jack's comments after the finish expressed his joy at winning this race, but he

The first version of the Jada 500 in the Hockenheim paddock in 1971.

also noted: "I had asked for help from Suzuki England, who agreed to lend me two 'factory' pistons as I was short of parts. I won, but after the race, they asked me to return the pistons as they were needed as spares for Barry Sheene's bike!" Further proof, if needed, that Jack always went his own way, knowing very well that he could only count on himself. And there's another nice little anecdote: after taking pole position in qualifying, Jack bet with his friend Tommy Robb that, if he won the race, he'd shave off his moustache, which happened immediately, since Tommy waited for him at the foot of the podium with a razor in his hand!

As the season drew to a close, Jack would finish fifth in the Italian GP at Monza and sixth in the Spanish GP at Jarama, good enough to resume a decent place in the World Championship table by ending up fifth overall, behind Agostini, Suzuki riders Turner and Bron, who were sponsored by their local importers, and his Kawasaki-mounted friend Dave Simmonds, winner of the final GP race of the year in Spain.

"Suzuki England ... agreed to lend me two 'factory' pistons ... but after the race, they asked me to return the pistons as they were needed as spares for Barry Sheene's bike!"

At Dan Hunt's request, in October Jack took part in the two-race Formula 750 250-mile event in Ontario, California, finishing 21st overall on his American sponsor's 350 Yamaha.

In November, I went to the Milan show, and stayed for a week with Jack and Nanou in their small apartment not far from Daniele Fontana's place. From this stay, I have photos taken at the brake factory and the workshop where Jack prepared his bikes, but I only have three blurry images taken in their home: one of Jack listening to music in an armchair, another of Nanou reading a newspaper, and one of myself taken by Nanou, who had come to surprise me in the folding bed reserved for their guests. From that moment on, my relationship with them grew stronger, even though I had known them for four years.

Four two-strokes and a solitary four-stroke on the front row of the 1971 Belgian GP in Spa: (front to rear) Jack, Christian Ravel, Dave Simmonds, Bo Granath and Giacomo Agostini.

While accompanying them to the show, I noticed how much Jack was loved in Italy. Among his close friends was the former rider-turned-journalist Roberto Patrignani, who clearly admired him greatly. Jack was respected by everyone, and it was evident that Fontana had displayed good intuition in choosing him as a development rider and flag-bearer for his brakes. Another loyal friend was Angelo Menani, a major accessories manufacturer whose workshop provided handlebars,

The furious battle between Ravel, Jack and Offenstadt during the 1971 Belgian GP in Spa ended tragically.

Dolce vita in the Imatra paddock in Finland, as Alberto Pagani cleans his Linto, beside Tommy Robb and his wife and an Australian friend.

brake levers, gear selector linkages, footrests, plastics of all kinds, tanks and fairings to the racing world. Menani remained a faithful supporter of Jack's for a long time.

At that moment, in Fontana's premises, I saw and photographed three different frames: the Cardani chassis, easily recognisable; the Jada frame used throughout the 1971 season; and a T500 Suzuki street frame, left over from the motorcycle whose engine they had used for the racer.

As soon as these social events were over, it was time to think about the 1972 season. To pursue his ideas, Jack had a new frame built, even lighter than the previous one, with thinner rear tubes, recognisable by the small vertical reinforcement strut running upwards from the swingarm pivot. Assembly and welding were again entrusted to the Beletti workshop. This second version of the Jada was the most refined, with the frame and swingarm assembly weighing less than 10kg, and the motorcycle ready to race at 115kg, lighter than a Suzuki TR500 or a Kawasaki H1R, its two main rivals. For the 350 class, Jack retained a TA350 Yamaha. He had sold his 250 as there were now plenty of machines in this category, which had become the entry point for young riders in Grand Prix, a class he now looked at with a certain amount of condescension and didn't want to compete in.

As usual, the winter passed quickly between long hours in the workshop, a tour of various suppliers, engine testing on the dyno and the ongoing assembly of the new bike. At the beginning of 1972, Jack and Nanou learned that *Continental Circus*, the film shot by Jérôme Laperrousaz three years earlier, would finally be released in cinemas in the spring, with the first public screening in Clermont-Ferrand, as a

The start of the 1971 500cc Ulster GP in Dundrod, with Jack leading on the Jada – and no Agostini!

preview before the French Grand Prix there in early May. In fact, Jack and Nanou had been invited to a private screening in Cannes a year earlier, but the film was then re-edited at the distributor's request.

"The first version we saw reflected the atmosphere of the Continental Circus better," Nanou would say later. "But for theatrical release, the film was shortened, and the dramatic side of the race was amplified, with that series of crashes at the beginning. Then the season's story highlights Jack's misfortunes, and gives me a role I would have preferred to avoid. Ultimately, it distorts Jack Findlay's image – he wasn't just that unlucky guy who always gets injured or breaks down."

Yes, but here's the thing: the success of *Continental Circus* was immediate. It won the Jean Vigo Prize at the Cannes Film Festival and appeared in the French film selection at the Oscars ceremony in Hollywood. It was acclaimed by motorcycle fans

Top left: Jack loved the true road racing tracks like the Irish ones, but they were really dangerous.
Above: Jack crosses the finishing line in Ulster to win his first 500cc World Championship race.
Left: The victorious Jack on the Ulster GP podium, with fellow Suzuki rider Dutchman Rob Bron second.

who saw Jack as the symbol of those two-wheeled adventurers, the lonely privateer rider competing against the factory teams. So much so that *Continental Circus* would become a cult movie, forever retaining the power of its images.

The film's release marked a new turning point in Jack's life due to the whirlwind series of promotions surrounding its launch. So, a completely crazy race was dreamed up, the so-called 'Prix de Paris', scheduled for late October, on a track set up in the access roads of the Rungis food market, near Orly Airport. Back in the spring, Jack and Nanou had met Sylvain Sanchez, the man who came up with this race to promote the film, and who would accompany them from circuit to circuit for a good part of the season.

At that time, the racing world in Europe was in turmoil. All eyes were on the 200 Miles of Daytona, where Japanese factories were competing, having abandoned Grand Prix racing in favour of the new Formula 750 category for tuned-up street bike engines in full race frames. In Italy, the Imola circuit organisers decided to set up a similar race, scheduled for early April, with huge prize money. Italian factories

In the first Imola 200 Miles race in April 1972, Jack rode a works Moto Guzzi 750 twin to tenth place.

In May 1972, Jack was back at Bourg-en-Bresse with a well-earned win in the 350 race in front of Frenchman Ramon Jimenez.

April 1972: Jack gives his new Jada its debut ride at the Nürburgring in the 500 German GP.

including MV Agusta, Ducati and Moto Guzzi were taking part, and the latter offered Jack the chance to ride one of their shaft-drive bikes. The prize money was great, the opportunity enticing, so for his first outing of the season Jack rode this big 750cc V-twin machine to an honourable tenth place. Back at the end of 1968, when he had explained his vision of what Grand Prix racing should become, Jack advocated a single top-level category, and in early 1972, everyone thought that Formula 750 would be exactly that.

Jack on the podium in Bourg after his 350 success.

The serious business began right after Imola, with the German GP at Nürburgring, where Jack finished seventh in the 500, then the French GP at Clermont-Ferrand, where he had two retirements. But the whole paddock was buzzing about this film the public had just discovered, and Jack found himself to be a movie star whether he liked it or not. In between two victories – one in the 500 at Hockenheim and the other in the 350 at Bourg-en-Bresse, setting a new lap record – the Italian GP at Imola was disappointing, with two more DNFs.

But there at Imola, Jack received good news: SAIAD, the Italian Suzuki importer, had just received from the Japanese factory one of the TR750s that were

Top left: Jack on his way to a third place in the Isle of Man aboard his Suzuki 750.
Top right: The 1972 Jada 500, seen here in Assen, is a fine testament to Jack's talent for building and preparing a bike.
Centre: The 1972 F750 TT race podium: Triumph works riders Ray Pickrell and Tony Jefferies, first and second, beside Jack, third on a Suzuki.
Left: Surprisingly, Jack rode a 125 Maïco two-stroke single in the 1972 Belgian GP in Spa.

Jack built his second Jada to suit his own personal build, so the bike was light and very easy to ride.

making a name for themselves in the US. The rider was supposed to be Guido Mandracci, but since he didn't want to race in the Isle of Man TT, the team manager offered Jack the bike for this race. It was no big coincidence, for that team manager was none other than Roberto Patrignani, Jack's great friend and a big fan of the British public roads race. The Suzuki factory, also eager to be present at the Isle of Man, supported this initiative. Jack finished third, behind the factory Triumphs of Ray Pickrell and Tony Jefferies. In the 350 Junior TT, he finished fourth after a good battle with fellow Yamaha riders Mick Grant and Tony Rutter, behind Agostini's MV. The latter had a new teammate in the 500 class, Alberto Pagani, making life harder still for privateers.

That year, the Tourist Trophy was marked by the fatal crash of Italian rider Gilberto Parlotti in the 125 race. As a result, Agostini and Phil Read publicly announced they would never return to this race. While British riders

Jack having fun on a 750 MV Agusta street bike while exploring the Rungis track in September 1972.

Jack follows his Kiwi friend Kim Newcombe's König 500 on the temporary Rungis circuit.

and journalists defend it unreservedly, French and Italian journalists, among others, joined the group of riders demanding its removal from the Grand Prix calendar. I was one of those, which led to many discussions with Jack, who believed we, the press, shouldn't get involved. He defended public road circuits like the TT, agreeing with the maxim that these 'separated the men from the boys'. During these discussions, he also told me that on a circuit like Assen, reputed to be so safe, there were actually ten times more crashes than at Spa, as this sense of security pushed riders to take too many risks. Behind this critique was also the fact that, with the arrival of the 250 and 350 Yamaha customer racers, more and more younger riders were applying for starts in the Grands Prix. In both categories, it was becoming increasingly difficult to finish on the podium, and Jack, like many veteran riders, didn't like it. He still scored points in the 350 at the Dutch and Swedish GPs, he scored good places and thus good prize money in International races, with occasional out-of-the-ordinary rides like a 125 start on a Maico in the Belgian GP, or a brief test session on the König of his friend Kim Newcombe at Tilburg in Holland.

Jack with his mother, who went to see him in Paris in September 1972.

In the 500cc class, it was as difficult as ever to aim for the podium behind Agostini. Jack would only manage it twice with the Jada, finishing second in Czechoslovakia and third in Spain, securing him ninth place in the 1972 World Championship. His popularity in France earned him a seat in the Bol d'Or 24-Hour race with the Kawasaki France team, riding alongside Jean-Claude Guénard, who'd started his career on motorcycles before moving to cars, and was riding bikes again.

During a final 750 race at the Paul Ricard Circuit in early October, Jack was able to ride SAIAD's TR750 Suzuki again, which allowed him to strengthen his ties with the team. Then came the infamous Prix de Paris at Rungis, which had a tremendous impact in France: a motorcycle rally was organised at the Eiffel Tower to announce the race, and marketing promotion was provided by the daily newspaper France-Soir and the radio station RTL. After more than six months in cinemas, the *Continental Circus* movie made Jack a modern-day hero, and there was a powerful buzz around the bike and our man.

Organiser Sylvain Sanchez asked me to help him follow Jack in preparing for the race. I attended the sighting laps of the Rungis track by Jack, aboard a 750 MV Agusta street bike and his Jada racer, under the eye of Sanchez's camera, capturing images which were widely distributed for the promotion of this fake Grand Prix, which was to take place on 22 October. In the run-up to this event, Jack brought his mother over from Australia, a long-held dream of hers.

The race meeting comprised a two-part 750 race, plus one each for 250s and sidecars as supporting acts. It was a fiasco from start to finish. The public had invaded the venue during the night, without buying tickets, the weather was gloomy and the track wet. Agostini, the star of the show, was eliminated by a fall on the first lap after being hit by another rider. The race was won by Dave Simmonds while Jack, who had hesitated making a choice between various bikes, finally started on a borrowed 350 Yamaha to honour his commitments to Sanchez. But he'd been injured already in a practice crash aboard the Jada, and did not finish the race, after another fall.

The day ended with a drama that traumatised the small world of the Continental Circus. That evening, Jack and Nanou were invited to a reception, and were going to stay in a hotel. His mother preferred to sleep in their caravan, in the paddock. That evening, having smelt something burning, she went to get Billie Nelson and Dave Simmonds, who were in caravans next door. A short-circuited light bulb had set the foam mattress on fire. Seeing this, Simmonds, who was bare-chested and wearing shorts, entered the caravan to throw a bucket of water on it. A chemical reaction caused an explosion in which he was seriously burned, and the caravan destroyed. Rushed to hospital in Clamart, Dave passed away two days later.

For Jack and Nanou, this tragedy was a terrible shock, bringing a dramatic conclusion to a turbulent year. The release of the film and the Rungis Festival had, despite himself, drawn Jack into a media spiral that was beyond his control. This stardom, which had both its good and bad sides, introduced an imbalance into his life and his relationship with Nanou, to the point of influencing the following years, and the end of his career.

It's show time for Jack, Barry Sheene and Olivier Chevallier on stage with the Crazy Horse Saloon dancers in Paris as part of the Rungis race publicity drive.

Continental Circus – The Movie

On its release in April 1972, *Continental Circus* captivated racing enthusiasts. It perfectly depicted the unique world where a group of nomadic riders travelled across Europe to race every Sunday in a different country. Shot in English, it also highlighted the significance of English speakers in this small world. "The Continental Circus was an Anglo-Saxon community where British, Australian, South African and New Zealand riders constituted a world of their own, and imposed their culture on it," said Italian rider Paolo Campanelli, who raced in it for several years. Laperrousaz's film accurately portrays this universe, where danger was omnipresent and fatal crashes frequent.

For Jack, it was the unflinching reflection of the harsh reality of racing: "Jérôme filmed my worst season, but everything is true in this film. When it was released, some people criticised its unduly harsh portrayal of our world. Because there were so many deaths, they didn't want to or

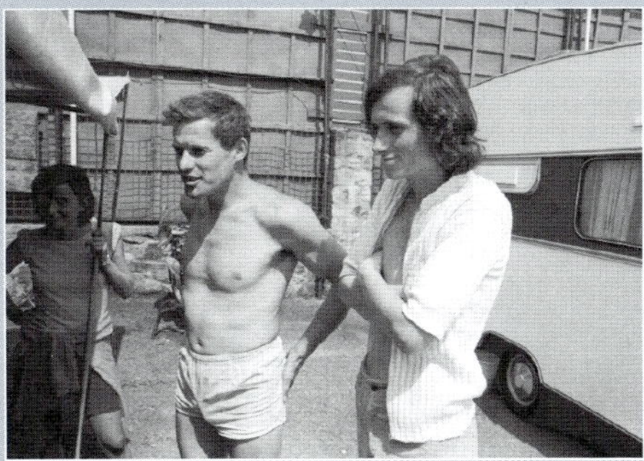

Jack with Jérôme Laperrousaz during the shooting of the film.

A test with a camera bolted to Jack's helmet.

couldn't understand that our daily lives also included muddy paddocks, noise, sweat, poverty for many, rain and blood," he confessed in an interview with Italian journalist Carlo Perelli.

Jérôme Laperrousaz added: "*Continental Circus* is a cult film because it reflects a bygone era. At the same time, rock 'n' roll stars were also dying young. They had their guitars, just as the riders had their motorcycles, to express a form of rebellion, a rejection of a cushy society. They'd rather die than go work in a factory. That's what I wanted to show, by transposing a sort of class struggle into this closed environment, between a private rider fighting for his existence, and a factory rider to whom everything is given."

The film crew with Jack under his truck's awning.

It was very difficult at the time to capture images on a moving bike.

Two bikes were used for shooting the movie, as seen here at Le Mans.

CHAPTER 7

Finally, a Factory Rider

1973-1974

This sad end to 1972 still finished on a positive note. Jack learned from Suzuki officials in Italy that the following year he would be fully integrated into their racing team alongside Guido Mandracci. Both men would each benefit from two true factory machines: a three-cylinder TR750 XR11 and a TR500 twin, but the latest XR05 model with liquid cooling. For the first time in his career, Jack would have a team of mechanics at his disposal. He wouldn't have to transport his bikes, resulting in racing conditions that were drastically different from anything he'd experienced.

Signing with Suzuki Italy had an unexpected consequence. The importer had an agreement with the French tyre manufacturer Michelin's Italian distributor, while at the same time Pierre Dupasquier, a young engineer, was fighting to create a competition service within the company. Michelin didn't yet have specific products for racing, but Dupasquier gambled that it could use the structure and design of the highest-performance road tyres combined with the most effective rubber compounds. Jack immediately agreed to race with these Michelin tyres. He believed in the development capacity of this brand, and remembering his years of struggle when he'd paid an unduly high price for his Dunlop tyres, or had to beg for free ones even as his record of success grew larger, he was not unhappy to see this manufacturer arrive. Michelin's race service in its early days was little more than rudimentary, with only one technician, Claude Decottignie, driving his small Citroën truck with a caravan. Because of budget constraints, he slept in the paddock, often accompanied by his wife. Jack and Claude quickly became friends, and while some French riders had already agreed to ride on Michelins, Jack was the first well-known foreign rider to do so.

Jack breezes to victory in the 1973 Senior TT aboard his Jada Suzuki 500 twin.

Confident now in the bikes at his disposal, since he knew their potential and had the support of a factory team, Jack didn't hesitate to sell the Jada and his 350 Yamaha. By focusing on the 750 class, and deciding to take part in Grand Prix races only in the 500 category, he was at the forefront of a movement that would soon become widespread, confirming that only those categories were of interest for a top-level rider.

Interesting, yes, but fiercely contested, because there were more and more factory bikes and many new riders. Early in 1973, Yamaha announced its big comeback with, for the first time, a four-cylinder 500 two-stroke in the hands of Jarno Saarinen and Hideo Kanaya, to challenge the MV Agusta four-stroke fours of Agostini and Phil Read. The 500 Suzuki was indeed a factory two-stroke bike, but it only had two cylinders, and could not compete in the battle of the four-cylinder bikes. But its presence marked a re-engagement of the Suzuki factory in road racing, so who knew what the future may hold.

The Italian Suzuki importer squad at Daytona in 1973: Jack's teammate is Guido Mandracci with, beside him, his friend Roberto Patrignani, the team manager.

The season would therefore revolve around the Formula 750 races, which were increasingly numerous throughout Europe, and the 500 Grand Prix races, which were predicted to be eclipsed by the 750 in the long run. The prestige of the Daytona and Imola 200-Milers with their colossal prize funds overshadowed Grand Prix racing, but in a sporting arena, you can't be sure of anything. Proof? The two races at Daytona and Imola were won by the Finn Jarno Saarinen on a 'small' 350 Yamaha, because while the true 750s had a clear advantage in power and speed, they lacked reliability. Forced to retire at Daytona, Jack was sixth overall in the two heats at Imola. Two F750 events in France allowed him to perform well, with a lap

The French 1970 season started in Rouen, where Jack's Suzuki leads Ron Chandler on a Triumph.

The works 500 Suzuki twin was released in 1969, but Jack got one only in 1973.

Top: The 1973 Senior TT winner in Victory Lane with Charlie Sanby (left) and Peter Williams. Left: Nanou with the signalling board. Beside her is Suzuki engineer and team manager Yasumori Kamiya. Right: A dream come true: Jack is awarded the huge trophy for his Senior TT win.

Jack in full flight on the Isle of Man TT's Mountain Course.

record at Rouen, and fifth place at Paul Ricard, in a race won easily by his teammate Mandracci.

In the French Grand Prix, the first of the season, he finished tenth. Jarno Saarinen, the winner, made a strong impression by completely dominating Agostini, who fell victim to a crash, then repeated his success at the Austrian GP eight days later. At the German GP, he was leading when his chain broke. This showdown between Yamaha and MV Agusta overshadowed the presence of the Suzukis in the category. When the Italian GP arrived at Monza, all attention was focused on the Italy–Japan confrontation, MV Agusta against Yamaha. Jarno Saarinen, now the superstar of the moment, also competed in the 250 World Championship. He had just won three GPs effortlessly and was the big favourite at Monza. But on the first lap of the race, the engine seizure of his main rival Renzo Pasolini's Aermacchi Harley-Davidson caused him to crash and take a dozen other riders down with him, including Saarinen. The bikes bounced off the guardrails lining the track, several of them caught fire, and the toll was dreadful. There were two fatalities: Saarinen, the reigning world 250 champion, and Pasolini, the vice-champion (by one point). Of course, the race was stopped and the Grand Prix cancelled.

This accident was a huge shock within the Continental Circus, reigniting the debate on circuit safety and exacerbating the division between young and old riders, between modernists and conservatives, of which Jack became one of the representatives. I talked to Jack after the Monza accident, and we had a big argument because Jack had coldly said to me, "When a rider dies, it could be a guy you really like, but it could also be a guy you don't like at all." This sentence revolted me, and we clashed on the subject of safety. He defended his vision of racing and circuits, the fact that a rider must adapt to the hazards of the track, and I said that I was fed up with

Barry Sheene in the 1973 F750 race in Hockenheim, with teammates Jack and Stan Woods protecting their team leader.

seeing friends of my age kill themselves. Just before Monza, the Frenchman André-Luc Appietto, whom I knew well, had been killed at Bourg-en-Bresse.

At the end of May, a new incident would widen the gap between the older riders and the younger generation. A Formula 750 race had been scheduled for Clermont-Ferrand. At the event, the French riders led a revolt to demand more safety measures and the protection of the metal guardrails with straw bales. The organisers promised to add more for the race, but by Sunday morning there were none, so the French decided to go on strike and not race. The paddock was divided into two, with almost all the English-speaking riders agreeing to race, including Jack, who became the chief target of the protesters.

Jack didn't care, as you can imagine. As soon as he'd finished the race in Clermont-Ferrand without scoring any points, he headed to the Isle of Man, where he was entered in both the 500 and 750 Tourist Trophy events. He was imperious in the Senior TT, dominating all his rivals aboard his Suzuki, averaging 163.42km/h (101.55mph), including two fuel stops, to win the six-lap race, much to the delight of the Michelin technicians, who advocated for the company's

The first appearance of the Suzuki RG500 square four at the 1974 French GP in Clermont-Ferrand.

Jack riding the RG500 Suzuki during the Senior TT.

entry into racing. Pierre Dupasquier would later say, "We fought to create this race service, and in the first year we did so. Findlay showed that we were right by winning the TT." To top it off, due to his French racing licence, it was the French national anthem that greeted his victory on the podium, not the Australian one!

"It was a perfect race, which went exactly as planned," recounted Jack. "The bike was a bit heavy because we'd fitted aluminium crankcases for extra safety, so it was fast, but the handling wasn't perfect. But since I was also riding the 750 at the TT that year, the 500 seemed easy handling by comparison."

In the F750 race, his Suzuki broke down while he was in second place, but he still had time to break the record for the highest speed yet recorded on the Mountain Course, achieving 264km/h (164mph) at the Highlander.

Back on the Continent, after retiring in the Yugoslavian GP, Jack finished fifth in the Dutch TT and third in the Belgian GP, behind the unbeatable MVs of Agostini and his new teammate, Phil Read. Two retirements in the following 500 GP races in Brno and Sweden were compensated for by a fine victory in the Swedish F750 round at the Anderstorp circuit, run on the same weekend as the GP, with a

In 1974 the prototype RG500 Suzuki square four was fragile and unreliable. Here, Jack leads Paul Eickelberg's König at Spa.

Jack and the three-cylinder Suzuki TR750 XR11. In 1974, he briefly enjoyed a full factory team riding contract with the Japanese manufacturer.

lap record to boot. Riding without any fuss, as always, Jack demonstrated that he knew perfectly well how to master this super-powerful bike, which American riders had nicknamed the 'flexi-flyer' thanks to its torturous handling. Shortly after, at Silverstone, he took second place with the big Suzuki in the overall results of the two F750 races. To top it off, at the request of Suzuki Italy, Jack and his teammate Guido Mandracci entered the 1000km endurance race at Imola, dominating on this 750 two-stroke – quite an achievement in durability.

A retirement in the final 500 GP of the season at Jarama in Spain didn't bother him much. The 500 Suzuki twin wasn't exactly a thunderbolt in terms of performance, even if its liquid-cooled engine was a little more powerful than the air-cooled Jada of previous years.

There were still two more Formula 750 races on the schedule, in Germany and Spain. Englishman Barry Sheene was in a position to win the championship riding a Suzuki, and his British team manager asked Jack to do everything he could to help him. Without being real teammates, Sheene and Findlay were riding for the same brand, on factory bikes, so Jack played the game. He won one race in Germany to beat Sheene's Yamaha-mounted rival, fellow Australian John Dodds, and finished fifth overall on combined results, then fourth in Spain on Barcelona's Montjuich Park circuit, where Sheene clinched the first European Formula 750 championship title. Jack ended up third in the final points standings.

All the Suzuki riders knew the factory was seriously considering becoming fully re-engaged in 500 Grand Prix racing, with the brand-new 500 square-four prototype. The choice of riders wasn't yet known, although it was obvious that Barry Sheene was first in line. But who would be his teammate? Jack relied on his contacts within Suzuki Italy to support him. He was assured of having a 750 at his disposal again and a liquid-cooled 500 twin. He could spend the winter in Milan relaxing, having very little to do – no bikes to prepare, no endless hours in the workshop. He took advantage of all the invitations to appear at winter shows and other such events in Italy and France. The Suzuki factory's decision would be known at the beginning of the year. They just had to wait.

With the arrival of a brand-new four-cylinder Suzuki 500, after the Yamaha of the previous year, 1974 would mark a revival of this category for factory riders. But for privateers, or the vast majority of the field, it would confirm a trend running counter to this revival. Their favourite 500 GP bike would be the smaller Yamaha TZ350, thousands of which were sold, and which could easily be made legal for the 500 category with a minor modification to increase the engine displacement by a few cubic centimetres. The superficial technical inspections at each race would favour the presence of this machine in a category where it didn't belong, with many riders content to enter a TZ350 and simply swap the race number backgrounds from blue (for 350) to yellow (500) just to collect their start money. This practice would cause friction between those who insisted on strict adherence to the regulations, and all those young hopefuls whose dream was to race in Grands Prix at minimal cost.

When the Suzuki factory finally announced its 1974 race programme, it was revealed that the two factory riders would be Britons Barry Sheene and Paul Smart. Jack would again be given a twin-cylinder bike, which was likely to be uncompetitive against the plethora of four-cylinder machines. But when he arrived at Clermont-Ferrand for the first GP of the season, he learned from his friend Roberto Patrignani, who accompanied the Suzuki Italy mechanics, that the Japanese engineers wanted to

Racing on open roads was natural at that time. Jumping the railway level crossing at Imatra, Finland.

Even with works bikes provided by Suzuki for the 1974 season, Jack often seemed troubled.

entrust him with one of the new four-cylinder bikes, to take advantage of his experience in speeding up its development. Ranged against them were two MV Agustas in the hands of reigning world champion Phil Read and teammate Gianfranco Bonera, and two Yamahas ridden by Giacomo Agostini – who was racing a two-stroke for the first time, after defecting from MV Agusta – and Teuvo Lansivuori.

With the Suzuki being brand-new, its riders knew that getting its setup right at each circuit would be difficult. Yet, from very its first race in France at Clermont-Ferrand, this all-new machine showed tremendous potential. Sheene finished second behind Read, with Jack 12th, hampered by an underperforming engine, while Smart retired. The next race was to be held on the Nürburgring circuit, but the crash of a rider during practice, who was injured after hitting the guardrails and took a long time to be evacuated, highlighted the track's safety deficiencies. Immediately, the factory riders, led by Agostini and Sheene, refused to start, bringing almost the entire field with them. The race was a sad farce, with only four completely unknown German riders at the finish.

In Austria eight days later, Sheene finished third and Jack fourth. The Suzuki was confirming its potential, and its riders began to think seriously about competing with the MVs and Yamahas. But the following races demonstrated that a new machine took time to find its rhythm. Barry Sheene fell victim to a crash after his engine seized in Italy, where Smart retired again, but Jack finished fourth.

> "On the wet tarmac, it was hell. The bike kept sliding, and I just couldn't accelerate as the rear wheel kept spinning."

Then came the Isle of Man TT, in which the British Suzuki importer, Suzuki GB, wanted the factory to take part. After much hesitation, Smart and Jack agreed to go. While Smart dominated F750 practice, Jack set the fastest time in the 500 class, just a few tenths off the lap record. But on race day, the weather was uncertain. It had rained just an hour before the start, so which tyres to use? "The Michelin technician had warned me: if the track continued to dry, a rain tyre wouldn't last a lap," said Jack. "So, I decided to start with a slick on the rear. But it started raining again shortly after the start." Smart quickly retired, while Jack struggled on with his slick rear tyre, which lost all grip. "On the wet tarmac, it was hell. The bike kept sliding, and I just couldn't accelerate as the rear wheel kept spinning." Cautiously, Jack decided to stop

While riding a works bike, Jack was nevertheless still a rather solitary privateer rider.

at the end of the first lap, while in the lead of the race. The TT isn't a place where you can take risks like that. However, the Suzuki GB management were furious, and blamed him for what they saw as an unjustified retirement.

In Holland, a fourth bike was made available, to Guido Mandracci. But none of the Suzuki riders would cross the finish line: Jack crashed unhurt, and his teammates all broke down. In Belgium, Sheene was faster than Jack in practice but didn't finish the race. In placing fifth, Jack scored points for the third time that season. He would do so again in Finland (fourth) and in Czechoslovakia (seventh), showing himself to be the best Suzuki rider in the final points table, taking fifth ahead of Barry Sheene, who had only finished three races.

His season in F750 on the three-cylinder Suzuki was less fruitful than the previous one. The newly created championship struggled to find its footing, with only three events counting towards the final standings. After a second place in Spain and a retirement in Sweden, Jack finished seventh in England. Those two results gave him third place in the final points table of a championship which had little value, not reflecting the growing enthusiasm for F750 racing, boosted by the arrival of a new customer racer, the Yamaha TZ700, which would go on to dominate the category.

As 1974 came to an end, with Jack having good cause to be optimistic that he'd be trusted again by Suzuki to race their bikes the following season, he instead took a hard hit: Suzuki announced it wouldn't renew his contract, and wouldn't give him any bikes for the 1975 season. "They never forgave me for stopping at the TT, but it was impossible for me to continue on slick tyres, and equally impossible to change wheels."

So everything had to be started all over again. Those two happy years were merely an interlude in the life of Jack, the eternal privateer.

Formula 750

From 1970 on, the American Daytona 200-Mile race in Florida each March gave a new impetus to motorcycle road racing. That year, a four-cylinder 750cc Honda won the race at the hands of Dick Mann. Honda had left Grand Prix racing at the end of the 1967 season, and its return to the race tracks with this bike gave a strong boost to the 750 category that had become established in the US. Suzuki, Kawasaki and Yamaha quickly followed suit. For nearly ten years, the Daytona 200 was the highest-profile race in the world. The International Motorcycling Federation/FIM, which governed global motorcycle sport, could not ignore this category, so it created the Formula 750 championship, which was contested from 1973 to 1980. However, while riders wanted a single-race formula to designate a single world champion, the parallel development of the 500cc category in which three of the four Japanese factories (excluding Honda) also invested took the focus back to this more traditional category.

Suffering from a lack of promotion and a clear set of rules, the 750cc championship was initially entitled the FIM Formula 750 Prize when established in 1973, before attaining World Championship status in 1977. However, the ultimate domination by one model (the Yamaha TZ750), and the increasingly popular Superbike four-stroke production-based class, meant the FIM discontinued the F750 class after the 1979 season. It was not until 2002 and the transition from 500 to MotoGP that Jack's long-standing wish came true, and a single category finally designated the best rider in the world.

The umbrella girls were yet to come but, meanwhile, the Champion Spark Plugs girls were quite popular.

CHAPTER 8

Crowned Champion but a Privateer Again

1975

When Jack learned that Suzuki had decided to dispense with his services it was a hard blow, as he had not expected it. He had hoped at least to retain the support of Suzuki Italy and keep a 500 and a 750 at his disposal. Suddenly, he found himself without any machinery at all.

A year earlier, thanks to his Suzuki contract relieving him of any financial concerns, Jack had made an old dream come true by buying a high-end sports car, a De Tomaso Pantera. Without hesitation, he sold it to finance his new season as a privateer. But it was very late in the day to order new machinery. All the new Yamaha models for customer riders were long since spoken for. But salvation fortunately came from his fellow Australian and good friend Kel Carruthers, a one-time companion in the Continental Circus. Carruthers had the good fortune to have a factory Benelli 250 four to race in 1969, with which he won the world title. He then moved to the US, where he raced for a few years before becoming a race engineer for Yamaha USA's Race Service Center. "Kel told me he could get me a new TZ750 Yamaha engine and a used chassis, as well as prepare an old 700 engine with 250 cylinders, so I could compete in the 500 GPs using the same bike." So that's what happened.

Rescued in the nick of time, just as he turned 40, Jack was forced to start the 1975 season with bikes he didn't know. His main sponsors were still Fontana, whose new disc brakes Jack would use for the first time, and Angelo Menani, the Milan accessories manufacturer. And, having reverted to being a simple privateer in Grand Prix racing, he was once again subject to the fluctuating income of start-money benefits negotiated race-by-race. So he bought a 350 Yamaha to improve his income by racing in two classes each weekend, whenever possible.

In 1975, Jack was back as a privateer, but still ready to fight.

Without any travel budget, there was no question of going to Daytona, which nonetheless was the opening round of the 1975 Formula 750 championship. Jack's season began in France, with three successive meetings at Rouen, Magny-Cours and Paul Ricard. The bikes were not top-notch. At Imola, which counted for the F750 championship, things started to improve, with fifth place overall thanks to finishing seventh and fifth in the two races. The non-championship International meetings may have been less prestigious, but the start money and cash prizes helped replenish the funds. A victory in 500 at Tubbergen and a third in the 750 at Chimay meant that, little by little, the development of the machines progressed, and the season's budget came into the black.

"I wasn't very happy to start the year on these bikes," Jack told me during that season, "but very quickly I got used to them, especially the 750, which I've prepared by following the factory's recommendations to the letter. I've got nothing but praise for the result. It's proved to be both efficient and reliable."

Then came the Grands Prix. It wasn't great. The cobbled-together 500 engine wasn't exactly a thunderbolt, but it wasn't very reliable either, failing to finish in Austria, Germany and Italy. During the season, Jack had two good 500 races, finishing third in Belgium and Finland.

An unusual incident tarnished the Imatra result. That year, there were five factory 500cc four-cylinder machines: Agostini's Yamaha, the MV Agustas of Read and Bonera, and the Suzukis of Sheene and Lansivuori. Privateers knew their chances of finishing on the podium were almost nil, but everyone had fun and, after a few laps on a dangerous circuit like Imatra, the finishing order was usually set early on. That day, at the last moment, Philippe Coulon, a young, almost unknown Swiss rider, managed to obtain a place on the grid for the 500 race, but without receiving any start money. Having only a TZ350, he'd resorted to the old trick of painting the number plates yellow, and had started with the firm intention of scoring points, as the only way to secure entries in subsequent Grands Prix. Focused on his task, he started very quickly, and found himself ahead of all the other privateers. The successive retirements of the two MVs and one Suzuki put him in third place a few laps from the end, just ahead of Jack, Chas Mortimer and Steve Ellis on 'real' 500s. On the last lap, Jack passed Coulon to take third place at the finish. In a French newspaper report it was written that Coulon had deliberately let Jack pass on the last lap, to avoid a protest. The said protest was lodged by Mortimer and Ellis, who got Coulon disqualified. But the reporter noted that, at the prize-giving ceremony, Jack was booed by the French members of the paddock. Nanou later reacted in a letter to the newspaper, but if the incident is worth reporting it's because it illustrates the atmosphere of the Grands Prix at the time, which often took place in a kind of joyful chaos that could become acrimonious. If Jack was targeted that day, it was because – owing to his CV, his position on track safety, and on maintaining circuits like the Tourist Trophy in the calendar – he embodied the contrast between the restless younger generation that emerged thanks to the abundance of Yamaha 250 and 350 customer racers, and the old guard who demanded respect for codes of conduct or even rules the younger generation deemed outdated.

It wasn't very pleasant, but with Nanou and mechanic Derek Booth as his only support, Jack continued to compete at each round without showing his true feelings. He was nevertheless quite upset, unable to understand why he was being labelled as a symbol of a bygone Continental Circus that

One chassis and two engines for two different classes, 500 and 750. All you have to do is to learn how to switch engines fast – and Jack and his mechanic Derek Booth had plenty of practice at that.

In 1975, Jack raced a 350 Yamaha again for start money.

In 1975, Jack the privateer constantly had to fight against works machines. Beside Suzuki, Yamaha and MV Agusta's works 500s came the works Kawasakis in both 750 and 500cc classes. Here's Jack in front of Mick Grant's 500 at the Belgium GP, and Grant's teammate Barry Ditchburn on the 750 in Sweden.

was suddenly deemed outdated. For all these reasons, his 1975 season reflected what the life of riders was like at the time. Taking into account all three classes he raced in, Jack started more than 40 races that year, given that the F750 championship races were held in two heats. A sort of routine evolved between the Grands Prix and the International races, where he would line up in 350 and 500 and the 750. Each time, he had to negotiate the start money figure, and queue up after the races at the organiser's office to collect the envelope containing the precious banknotes that allowed him to continue. Despite those constraints, more and more young riders tried their luck in GP racing.

With ever more competition due to the mass arrival of the 350 Yamahas – those over-the-counter racers which had to be maintained by the rider himself – genuine spare parts were hard to find, and there were things to regret compared with previous seasons. But Jack, typically, was never one to complain about adversity, or to look back.

An invitation to the TT – to ride an 850cc Norton for the factory team in the Unlimited category – offered a chance to try something different. But, sadly, the ignition failed on lap 1 soon after the start.

In the midst of this chaos, Jack knew his best chances still lay in Formula 750 races. They were long, with each round held over two heats of 160km (100 miles) each, with World Championship points awarded on the basis of the combined overall results, so if you broke down in one heat or the other, you lost everything. It was in this category that he did best, scoring points six times out of the nine races on the schedule.

He couldn't compete at Daytona due to lack of budget, and was a victim of retirements at Anderstorp in Sweden and Hämeenlinna in Finland. But he was fifth

Two postcards showing how popular Jack was in that era.

in Imola, third in Mettet, and fourth in Magny-Cours. Each time, the competition was tough, with the works Suzukis of Barry Sheene, John Williams and John Newbold, but also factory Kawasakis ridden by Mick Grant, Barry Ditchburn and Canadian Yvon Duhamel. At Silverstone in August, Jack was fifth, then in early September at Assen in Holland, he finished second behind Duhamel's Kawasaki. On the eve of the final race in Germany, Sheene, who had won three races, led the championship by four points ahead of Jack. But Barry got injured in a paddock incident in Britain, so couldn't race in the final event at Hockenheim. Suzuki GB sent three machines entrusted to Stan Woods, Newbold, and Williams to defend its and Sheene's chances by blocking Jack. In the first heat, our man was third behind two of the three British Suzukis. In the second race, German Dieter Braun, who had relegated him to fifth place, broke down right at the end. Phew! By finishing fourth in the heat, Jack duly clinched the Formula 750 title by a single point, 46-45 ahead

No big sponsor's name on the fairing means a reduced budget and hard times.

of Sheene under the system then in force, with a rider's best five results counted for his final total. That came after finishing third overall on the day, with third in the first race and fourth in the second – although, if not for second-placed Philippe Coulon running out of fuel in race one after pitting with a faulty fuel filler, he would not have been champion. But, by depriving Suzuki of a second successive FIM F750 title, Jack provided the right kind of payback for their decision to drop him.

Jack was deeply upset when a number of journalists, mainly in France and Italy, devalued his title because he won it without any race victories. "When I crossed the

Wearing unlucky thirteen in Holland – but Jack wasn't superstitious.

The final 1975 F750 round in Germany, and Jack fights for the title against John Williams' works Suzuki.

finish line at Hockenheim, I thought about all those factory bikes and what they cost. I was criticised for not winning a single race. But the factory bikes I faced had exhaust systems that gave them 8 or 10 more horsepower than mine. Why did they expect me to win races against them?" As he finished his 16th Grand Prix season, with that win in the 750 series and a tenth place in the 500, Jack could look back on all the sacrifices, the perseverance and the determination that kept him from ever getting discouraged and allowed him to continue on this path.

"Starting in 1975, I was lucky to have an exceptional mechanic by my side: Derek Booth. I trusted him; he was precise and meticulous. He relieved me of many tasks. With Nanou handling the paperwork, as usual, I could focus better on the details, and my role as a rider. It was a particularly pleasant season."

The podium in Germany, and Jack is definitively crowned as the 1975 F750 champion.

Jack – by himself

Shortly after this last race, I conducted a long interview with Jack that was published in *Moto Journal*. It deserves to be in this book.

Q. Giacomo Agostini has been racing for over ten years, yet he wins a world title every year. You, Jack Findlay, waited 20 years for such an honour. How did you keep going for so long?
A. You must simply love riding motorcycles. You have to be passionate about them, and think of nothing else. After five or ten years, it's normal to get tired. Riders who have done it all and won everything get tired, and leave the sport. I'm still passionate because I'm searching for something in racing, though I'm not sure what exactly.

Q. What do you mean?
A. The things I strive to do, maybe it's about winning in my own way. This year I won – no, you can't say I won – I finished first in the F750 series, and that's something I've always dreamed of, of winning a championship with a bike I built myself. This year, I almost achieved it with a standard Yamaha that's mine, which I prepared myself. These are the dreams I aim to make come true. Like when I won the Ulster Grand Prix with the 500 Jada. It was my bike. Moments like that make all those years of struggles and problems worth it. That's my personal pleasure, that's what I seek in motorcycles. I'm very selfish, a lone wolf.

Q. Your troubles lasted for years. That's a lot, considering the satisfactions received.
A. No, you can't think like that. I've been racing for 25 years, but I hate talking about someone's age, because I believe you should focus on what someone is doing now, not what they've done in the past. I never think about what I've done, but always about what I'm going to do. The past is the past. At Hockenheim, I finished the race, they told me I was third, congratulations, you won. For me, at that moment, it was already over. With my friend Daniele Fontana, the brake manufacturer, we returned to Milan, put the engine on the bench, it made 108 horsepower, and we thought it wouldn't be enough for 1976. Then we reassembled the bike to go testing at the Paul Ricard Circuit with Michelin. A week after the last race, we were already working for the next season.

Q. But aren't you tired of being a privateer rider?

A. It doesn't bother me to ride for myself alone, but people don't have an accurate idea of what it is, and mistakenly call too many riders 'privateers'. Privateer riders are those who buy their bikes at the beginning of the season, then they might round up some small sponsorship for leathers, helmets or sparkplugs, but they pay for their bikes themselves. It's nothing like riders who are provided with bikes at the start of the season, riders who race for an importer, who might have a bike identical to mine, but have many more possibilities to make it go faster with factory assistance.

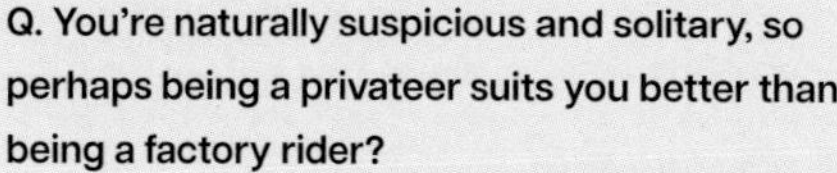

Q. You're naturally suspicious and solitary, so perhaps being a privateer suits you better than being a factory rider?

A. It's true that I trust only myself. Until not so long ago, I had no trust in other people. I was alone in racing, and did everything myself. But I hadn't had the opportunity to see others at work. In the Suzuki importer's team in Italy, there were mechanics who weren't really qualified. But later, when I worked with the factory team, I worked with Japanese mechanics. With them, there are never any problems, and I started to trust other people's work. I also learned to manage others, to tell them what I wanted them to do. Now I can stay calm, give instructions to a mechanic and supervise his work. It's better that way.

Q. But when you were a factory rider, were there any constraints you didn't handle well?

A. I was never really a factory rider, because being a true factory rider means collaborating with the engineers to develop the bike during the winter, not waiting until spring to test a ready-made machine. I like to be there, helping to build the bike, because I believe a rider is more complete if he knows his machine well. With a serious factory, the 1976 model should already be running in 1975. Formula 1 teams have already tested the cars for the following season, but

in motorcycles, there's nothing like that. The machines arrive more or less ready just in time for the first race of the season. I'd like to be part of a well-funded private team, so that the bikes would be ready at the start of winter, so we could ride them for the next four months, and then when the season came, we'd have had time to test everything, compare and contrast different solutions, and the team of mechanics would know exactly what to do in any situation.

Q. Is that what you did with Fontana when building the Jada?
A. Yes, but Daniele and I are too perfectionist. We spent the whole winter working on the bike, and sometimes went too far.

Q. Are you a perfectionist, a purist?
A. If that's what a purist is, then I'm a purist. When my bike is finished and ready to race, I don't like the line of the fairing, so I think we can do even better. This year, I fought against this tendency by buying a standard bike and forcing myself to make only essential modifications. My TZ750 remained original all year, and it's still the best system for a private rider.

Q. And with this standard bike, you won the equivalent of a World Championship.
A. In a way – I beat the others. I didn't win a race, but I won the championship. In fact, we were the best team, which made the best calculations by finishing more races than the other teams. It's not me who won the championship, but my team. The F750 races are high-speed endurance racing. I like this format of two 100-mile heats, each of which pose new problems. For spectators, it makes two interesting races, and they immediately understand who won. I'm talking about the general public, not the motorcyclists. It's this public that provide the revenue for us to go racing, but don't understand anything when they watch a Grand Prix event. They see six

different winners who never raced against each other. In Formula 750, there's a final outcome where one man comes out victorious.

Q. There are still people who think you were very lucky, and that it's not glorious to be a champion without winning a single race.

A. They say that behind my back, but don't have the courage to tell me to my face. If they did, I'd burst out laughing. The rules say that I'm the champion. You can't change them by saying Findlay doesn't deserve this title. In 1969, with the factory Linto, I kept breaking down even though I was always running second behind Agostini. Nobody came to sympathise with me. I know both sides of the coin.

Q. 1969 is the year covered by *Continental Circus*, the movie by Jérôme Laperrousaz. What do you think of it?

A. That film is the truth; that's what really happened. When we started, Jérôme didn't know where he was going, and neither did I. But I don't like watching that film, because I find it bad to dwell on the past.

Q. Laperrousaz focuses a lot on the bad luck that seems to dog you. Do you believe in this luck, in destiny?

A. I think I believe in destiny. For years I've tried to change my life, and you've seen all the trouble that brought me. Now I take life as it comes. If there's a bad moment, I tell myself it will pass. I'm an Aquarius, and my life is full of ups and downs. I let myself rise and fall with the waves. If I'm up, it's great; if I'm down, I just wait for it to pass.

Q. So, dying or getting killed in a race, is that an up or a down?

A. Death, dying, I don't think about that. I hope I'll be on a high when it happens. When you die, snap, it's over, done. So, if you're in a bad spot, with no money, no

friends, and you're going to die, oh no, that's too sad. But I never think about that. You can die at any moment. Look, our job is known to be dangerous. That's why riders try to live at a hundred per cent. Dying in a race, okay, but it's not something I think about.

Q. Is that why you defend the so-called natural circuits, why you love racing at the Tourist Trophy? Don't you have any concerns?
A. No, I don't think like that. I race on any circuit, because to me, they're all dangerous. I approach each circuit with the same mindset, to perform as well as I can, without making any mistakes. It might sound pretentious, but I think I am capable of doing that, of racing on difficult circuits. People might say that Findlay is bold or stupid to think he can do that, but it's true, I believe it. And I think all racers feel the same deep down, otherwise they wouldn't race. A track is always a track. It has curves of a certain shape. During practice, you study the technique needed to navigate each curve with the problems it presents. For me, the track is there, that's all. The presence of a tree or a wall is automatically factored into my calculation for taking the curve. At that limit, the bike moves and you know that if you risk going any faster, there's that wall. So, you don't take the risk. On a bike, you know that mistakes can be very costly. And that's why I love motorcycle racing: it's the only job where you can't make mistakes because your life is at stake. A head of state can make mistakes, which might cause others to die – but not him, he stays alive. Everything becomes
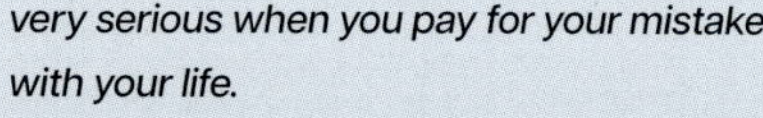
very serious when you pay for your mistake with your life.

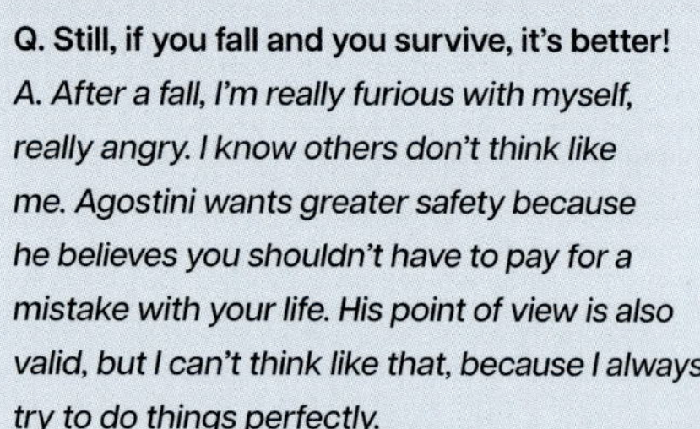
Q. Still, if you fall and you survive, it's better!
A. After a fall, I'm really furious with myself, really angry. I know others don't think like me. Agostini wants greater safety because he believes you shouldn't have to pay for a mistake with your life. His point of view is also valid, but I can't think like that, because I always try to do things perfectly.

Q. What extra factor does a circuit like the Isle of Man TT bring?
A. We need all types of circuits. I'm a specialist in high-speed circuits. At Magny-Cours, Paul Ricard, Spa- Francorchamps, you encounter different layouts, and become a complete racer.

For me, it's fascinating how each circuit poses specific problems, and you need a computer in your head to use all the knowledge acquired on every circuit to solve each problem. By eliminating the so-called dangerous circuits, we're moving towards the same type of layout everywhere, whether in Germany, the Netherlands, or Italy. So, why travel so much? One race would be enough to designate the world champion, since all circuits would be the same.

Q. What do you think has changed the most since you started racing?
A. The biggest change is the bike and its performance. It's improved by 100 per cent since I began, and everything else has followed from that. Before, in the 500cc class, we had 50 horsepower. Now, you need 100bhp to win, and at least 85 to be competitive. Everything has evolved: frames, brakes, suspensions, tyres. This increase in power has forced factories to find more capable riders, and thus pay them very well. Money has become more and more important with all the contracts, so that a well-paid rider gets used to a good standard of living. He continues to go fast, but understands he can lose everything in an instant. But he has to keep going to make more money. He's on the razor's edge, and acutely aware of it. If he crashes, he loses everything, but he also loses everything if he goes slower. So, he looks around the circuit and thinks about clearing up the surroundings of the track. In fact, everything happens in his head because things are what they are, and don't change. But it's due to this tremendous increase in power that we've arrived at this point.

Q. You're a solitary person by nature, but also increasingly isolated. Young riders don't think like you, and many of your friends like Billie Nelson or Dave Simmonds have disappeared.
A. Solitude doesn't bother me. I often like to be alone. Anyway, a rider is always alone even if he talks to everyone, even if he has lots of buddies. I've had a few friends, and it always hurts a lot when a friend disappears. So maybe it's better not to have too many friends.

The omnipresent factories

Jack's career, highlighted by *Continental Circus*, showcased the role played by factories in the World Championships created by the FIM in 1949, depending on whether they took part in them or not. In the 1950s, British, Italian and German factories were involved, then in the following decade, it was the turn of the Japanese manufacturers. After a brief interlude where they did not directly enter any teams, these same Japanese factories began reinvesting massively in the World Championships from 1975 on. Since then, Honda, Suzuki, Yamaha and Kawasaki never ceased to be present in motorcycle road racing in varying degrees of intensity. And since the advent of the MotoGP category in 2002, the Italian factories Ducati and Aprilia have also reinvested in competition. A Teutonic presence, so timidly represented by BMW in the 1950s, is now ensured by the Austrian KTM brand. Parallel to the MotoGP category, the FIM organises World Championships in the Superbike and Supersport categories, which now play a similar role to Formula 750, as in the era when Jack raced, by trying to field bikes closer to production models than the pure prototypes of MotoGP.

Five works bikes on the front row at the 1974 Finnish GP in Imatra: Read (1) and Bonera (11) with MVs, Lansivuori's Yamaha (21), Findlay's Suzuki (4), and Frenchman Leon's Kawasaki (14). Apart from George's self tuned four-cylinder Yamaha (5), all other bikes are 350 TZ Yamahas.

CHAPTER 9

End of Career

1976-1978

Reading Jack's interview after winning the Formula 750 European Championship explains everything. He harbours no illusions about what this success means and shows no signs of excitement. He only thinks about continuing to live for and live through his passion, albeit with some concerns. Gradually, not only because he was the oldest rider still competing, but also due to the influx of very young rivals (the 1975 350 world champion, Johnny Cecotto, was only 19), he began to be nicknamed 'Old Jack' in the paddock. This infuriated him: "I hate being called that. It's a way of making me look at the past. A rider's age doesn't matter; what counts is what he does in the present day, not the past." Another time he told me, "I don't like 'Old Jack' because I've already heard it being used about my mate, Jack Ahearn. It's demeaning. Eventually, he had trouble getting starts, and was offered less and less start money."

As always at the end of the season, the question arose: "What will I ride next year?" Thanks to his connections in Italy, he had the opportunity to test a prototype 500 parallel-twin with four carburettors being developed by the Aermacchi H-D factory racing team, based in Varese, north of Milan. But this test led nowhere. Jack didn't even try to get a 350, deciding to only race in two categories: the 500 in Grand Prix and the 750, where races were numerous, whether or not they counted towards the F750 European Championship. In this category, he decided to continue with his Yamaha from the previous year, which received a new engine, again provided by his friend Kel Carruthers, now firmly at the helm of the Yamaha USA team. But that 750 wasn't really satisfactory. He slightly modified the rear section in the hope of improving the handling. But after the Tourist Trophy, he decided to acquire a frame built by Nico Bakker in the Netherlands.

Mechanic Derek Booth spanners a second-hand Yamaha 750 for the 1976 season's opening race at Paul Ricard circuit.

For the 500 category, the choice was obvious. At the beginning of 1976, the Suzuki factory put the four-cylinder RG500 on sale, a competitive 500 derived from the factory prototype which debuted in 1974 and revolutionised Grand Prix racing's premier class, as it was the first time such a high-performance machine was ever offered in such large numbers to customer teams and riders. Since it was available from Suzuki distributors in Europe, a large number of them were seen at the starting

This picture, taken during the early-season Paul Ricard race, shows that the Yamaha TZ750 frame has been modified.

line from the first Grand Prix of the 1976 season at Le Mans. It brought about the same transformation to the 500 category as the Yamaha 250 and 350 had done in the smaller-capacity classes. In its first year, several dozen were sold, and immediately the Suzukis in the hands of privateer riders began dominating the leaderboard in races, behind the company's factory-supported star rider Barry Sheene, and his teammate John Williams.

Like around 20 other privateer riders, Jack succeeded in acquiring one of these new Suzukis. Theoretically, he should have had an advantage over the other customers, since he'd ridden the very first RG500 prototype produced by the factory

For the first 500 GP of the 1976 season, Jack is riding an over-the-counter Suzuki RG500, the same as around 20 other privateer riders.

In the 1976 500cc Swedish GP, Jack is seen leading a 350 Yamaha and South African Alan North on another RG500 Suzuki.

two years earlier. In fact, that experience wasn't much use to him, since a competitive RG straight out of the crate requires meticulous preparation and tuning work he had to learn, just like other tuners of the same bike. Remember that he rode it before for the factory team, so he didn't have to get his hands dirty working on the bike.

At the last moment, Angelo Menani and Fontana offered to provide him with a Yamaha 350. Jack wasn't keen on racing in this category, where over 100 riders were trying to get qualifying slots every weekend, but he eventually accepted the offer. His status as a privateer required him to make as many starts as possible. Moreover, Fontana had been manufacturing disc brakes for two years, and he needed Jack to test his products, to help improve them and, above all, to promote them in the paddocks, for competition was tough.

The season began with some Formula 750 races, where he didn't shine, and then the Grand Prix season started on 25 April at Le Mans. Jack failed to qualify in the 350, and retired after a breakdown in the 500. He scored points for the first time with his Suzuki 500 in the Austrian Grand Prix, finishing eighth, after a discreet 17th place in the 350. Skipping the F750 round in Spain for a lucrative International race in Hockenheim, he won in the 500 and finished sixth in the 350. The Italian Grand Prix at Mugello was a nightmare; there were so many contenders in the 350 that he failed to even qualify. In the 500, he was ninth on the grid but did not finish the race.

True to his principles, Jack went to compete at the Tourist Trophy, where he finished eighth in the 350, but retired in the 500, as well as in the 1000, where he'd started with his TZ750 Yamaha. It was the last time the TT counted towards the World Championships. From the following year, the British Grand Prix was staged at the Silverstone circuit, after a request from the riders calling for the TT to be discontinued for safety reasons. Jack's presence on the Isle of Man that year and his ardour in defending this race were an additional point of friction with the younger riders, who accused him of being backward-looking.

In this shot taken at the 1976 F750 Finnish round, we can clearly see the Suzuki's Bakker frame made in Holland, and the replacement Fontana disc brakes.

Fortunately for his morale, and especially his wallet, after two good F750 races at the Norisring near Nuremberg, where he debuted his new Yamaha chassis, Jack finished fifth in the Dutch TT, and second at the 500 Swedish Grand Prix behind Barry Sheene, the dominant force of the season destined to be crowned world champion later that year. In the final championship standings, with an additional seventh place in Finland, Jack finished eighth, just behind Agostini, who won the

Jack finished second at the 1976 F750 Silverstone race on his Niko Bakker-framed TZ750 Yamaha.

In 1976, the Belgian F750 round was organised on the Nivelles circuit.

Two shots from the 1976 Bol d'Or at Le Mans where Jack rode a works Honda RCB to fourth place with Stan Woods.

final Grand Prix in Germany on an MV Agusta. Ahead of them, there were only Suzukis.

But for Jack, that summer was mainly marked by a personal tragedy, which passed almost unnoticed amid the tumultuous brotherhood that was the Continental Circus. In August, Daniele Fontana died suddenly of a heart attack – a severe blow for Jack, who lost his dearest friend, and also a highly skilled technician. Daniele indeed provided multifaceted support. During their long collaboration, he was as comfortable taking exhaust measurements and drawing them as he was calculating the resistance of metals and the diameters of tubes needed to make a chassis, or any other metal part. "He was an exceptional man because he was as sharp-minded as he was skilled with his hands. He could sketch a drawing, calculate the resistance of steel, but he also excelled on a lathe or milling machine," Jack told me after his passing.

In the F750 category, the season was much less fruitful than the year before. Jack only scored points twice: tenth place in Italy and 12 points for the second place at Silverstone. Breakdowns and crashes followed one another. Despite some good results in International races, completing the season was difficult. "In some races, they offered me start money equal to what they offered me ten years ago with the Matchless." Faced with this ruthless system, Jack developed a strong aversion to Grand Prix organisers like those in Holland or Germany, who made huge profits without passing any of them on to the riders. This injustice caused him a strong resentment towards them until the end of his life.

His finances were quite low by the end of August. Fortunately, an offer from Jean-Louis Guillou, the manager of the Honda endurance race team, provided some relief. Honda had re-entered endurance racing earlier that year

Assen, September 76: Jack during the Champions Parade before the F750 race.

Waiting for a practice session to start at the 1977 Austrian GP. Jack is surrounded by three reporters: Italian Nico Cereghini, Briton Chris Carter and Jacques Bussillet.

with a new prototype, the RCB 1000. For the Bol d'Or 24-Hour race, to make a statement, Honda requested Guillou to field four bikes on the grid. This led Jack and his teammate Stan Woods to secure fourth place on the Bugatti circuit at Le Mans – a more than honourable result.

The first winter without Fontana by his side was particularly tough, exacerbated by strained relations with Nanou. Nonetheless, Jack embarked on the 1977 season with his Suzuki RG 500 and the Yamaha TZ750 with its Nico Bakker frame. Without sufficient start money to cover travel expenses, he had to miss out on competing in the Daytona 200 and the first Venezuelan 500 GP.

At the first Grand Prix in Europe, at the Salzburgring in Austria, a mass crash resulting in the death of Hans Stadelman prematurely ended the 350 race. Most 500 category riders protested against the disastrous safety conditions and initially refused to race. However, Jack and a few others agreed to start, with Jack winning the race convincingly on his Suzuki ahead of five similar privateer machines. It was his third Grand Prix victory, albeit under controversial circumstances which

The inglorious start line of the 1977 Austrian GP. The front line is empty thanks to a riders' strike after the multiple crash in the 350 race. Virginio Ferrari (28) is on the third row, while Jack (8) on the fourth will be the winner.

permanently ostracised him in the paddock.

We argued that day, and Jack sharply put me in my place. "What business is it of yours? Neither you nor any journalist, nor any other rider has the right to teach me any lessons. Year after year, I pay my own expenses in taking part in races. I pay for everything – my bikes, my mechanics, my truck and my travel expenses. I start each new season not knowing if I'll have enough money to finish it. So leave me alone. I need my start money and I need my prize money. No one has the right to

Jack and his Nico Bakker-framed Suzuki devoid of any sponsorship for the French GP early in 1977.

Top: Jack and Ferrari at the hairpin in Spa at the 1977 Belgium GP.
Centre: At the end of the 1977 season, the 750 Yamaha-Bakker wears the colours of a new sponsor.
Bottom: A bad weekend for Jack at the Mosport race in Canada, with mechanical troubles in practice and during the race.

tell me what to do, especially not guys backed by big sponsors who can break or smash as many bikes as they like, which someone else is paying for."

This was one of the few times I saw Jack genuinely angry, not just at me, but especially at all those people who had dared to judge him, to reproach him for not supporting the other riders.

Fifteen days later, after an uneventful weekend at the German GP, Jack had a big crash at the Imola circuit. Suffering from a head injury and, most critically, cardiac arrest, he was miraculously saved by Doctor Claudio Costa. Claudio, son of the race organiser at the circuit, had recently established a medical facility specialising in motorcycle trauma at the Faculty of Medicine in Bologna. He pioneered trauma treatment on the tracks, and with the help of AGV helmets, he created the first Clinica Mobile dedicated to motorcycle competition, an institution which endures today and ensures the presence of specialist doctors at all circuits.

Jack didn't let his Imola crash stop him from participating in the following two Grand Prix races, but he was in far from his best form. That was evident in his performance at the Tourist Trophy, where two of his three starts ended in retirement. But averaging 168.31km/h (104.58mph) – including two fuel stops to finish in sixth place behind winner Joey Dunlop on the Bakker-framed TZ750 Yamaha in the six-lap Formula Libre Jubilee TT, celebrating the 70th anniversary of the TT races – was a fine achievement in Jack's twilight years in racing. Moreover, the Tourist Trophy prize money was better than in previous years, and Jack really needed it.

He still managed to finish ninth in the Belgian GP in early July with his Suzuki which, like the 750, was then equipped with a Nico Bakker frame. But he didn't score any more points after that, with a 14th place in Sweden not offering much consolation, nor an eighth place in the final Formula 750 race in Germany. It concluded a disastrous season that could be summed up by a remark from one of his competitors, Frenchman Hubert Rigal: "In August, we had the Formula 750 round at Zolder in Belgium. After a crash, I was lying on a stretcher in the hospital near the circuit waiting for X-rays. They brought in another guy, not looking very fresh, and placed his stretcher next to me. It was Jack, who looked at me and said, 'You know, we really chose a job for idiots to do!'"

Having lost his Segura Leathers sponsorship, Jack had trouble finding a new leather company to support him in 1977.

Nevertheless, doing this 'idiotic job' was ingrained in all the riders, such was their passion for the sport. They were ready to endure anything to continue racing. Despite start money that barely covered their expenses, even after the organisers of two F750 races at Mosport in Canada and Laguna Seca in California had combined their budgets to finance transporting the bikes, a majority of riders made the journey, including Jack, who suffered repeated mechanical failures in both races. But missing out on any chance to race was out of the question, so in the final round of the F750 championship at Hockenheim, Jack finished 13th in the first race, tenth in the second, and eighth overall.

For many observers, including close friends, the 1977 season seemed like one season too many for Jack. Yet, deaf to all advice and hints

For the 1978 opening race of the season in Imola, Jack was riding a brand-new TZ750 Yamaha. Note the full-face helmet that he finally tried in practice.

Jack started the 1978 season with a brand-new RG500 Suzuki as well.

about his personal situation and age, he decided to continue into 1978. At 43, he was the elder statesman of a pack that had grown significantly younger. Few paid him any attention, but he didn't care. He sold off his ageing machines and bought two new models, a Suzuki RG 500 and a Yamaha TZ750, an investment that again ate into his meagre capital. He had a few small sponsors, but it didn't amount to much.

In his first 750 race of the season at Imola, after finishing an anonymous 30th in the first race, Jack suffered a serious crash in the second race caused by the rear wheel breaking up. Again suffering from a head injury, he was in a terrible state upon leaving the hospital. But he had no choice; he had to go to the next race. It was the Moto Journal 200, another F750 race, at the Paul Ricard Circuit. Jack managed to take part in practice, barely qualifying for the race. But François Chevallier, the circuit director, was aware of his condition, and went to him to say, "Listen, Jack, you're not fit to ride. Here's your prize money, on one condition: you don't start the race."

Jack followed his advice. Indeed, he was not fit to race. But he persisted, and he was on his way to the Isle of Man and its Tourist Trophy. Since their race had lost its World Championship status, the organisers offered serious start money to riders in an effort to maintain its reputation. That year, 1978, they even convinced Mike Hailwood to make a return. Jack barely saw any of it: "I was in a complete fog, sleeping 20 hours a day. I don't even know how I managed to go there, take part in practice and start the race. It was madness," he recounted later.

The rest of the season followed suit. Jack dragged himself from circuit to circuit, languishing at the bottom of the rankings whenever he chanced upon finishing a race. He scored no points in either the 500 or 750 categories. On 20 August, mounting a 500 for the 200th time, he lined up at the start at the Nürburgring, the same circuit where he contested his first Grand Prix in 1958, 20 years earlier. He finished the race in 14th. This led him to tell Don Cox long afterward, "I ran my first and last Grand Prix on the same circuit. With 20 years apart, I finished roughly in the same position. It proves I haven't progressed much!"

Hockenheim 1978, one of Jack's last races before he retired.

Yet, this wasn't the final race of his career. In early September, he was at Assen on his 750 Bakker-Yamaha where, after finishing 16th in the first race, he didn't complete the second. When he packed up his gear to head back to Italy, he was worn out, mentally, physically and, above all, financially. No one was waiting for him there anymore. After the passing of Daniele Fontana, he had lost his logistical base at his factory. Nanou had already told him she was moving to Nice, so now he was more alone than ever.

The athletes' tragedy

Ending a career is always a double tragedy for a great athlete. First, a moral and passionate drama, because they have to leave behind an activity that consumed all their time and energy for years, driven by their passion. But it can also be a social and financial drama for many, as ceasing to take part in the sport, however lucrative, forces them into an often difficult transition. The world of motorcycle racing allows for advertising brands or products, as it is directly linked to markets. This is why many riders have reinvented themselves as representatives for accessory brands, lubricant products or tyres and suchlike. It's no coincidence that Jack's second life involved testing tyres for Michelin, a brand that was grateful to have given him his first victory in the premier 500 GP category.

CHAPTER 10

Nanou, the Legendary Companion

It's impossible to devote a biography to Jack without mentioning Nanou, his partner who stood by his side from 1962 to 1978, experiencing all the most intense moments of his career.

I met Nanou in 1968, in circumstances that speak to her generosity. I went to the Italian Grand Prix with a friend. Upon arriving at Monza, we wanted to visit the paddock, but it was surrounded by high fences and well guarded. As we wondered how to get in, seeing Nanou on the other side of the fence, I called out to her, asking if she could get us in, saying we were fans of Jack. She came to us, then told us to wait for her a little further along the fence. Quietly, she slipped us two passes, asking us to come to her immediately to return them. In two minutes, we went to the paddock entrance, showed our cards, and returned them to Nanou, thanking her. And we remained friends forever. The generous Nanou was never stingy with a cake or a cup of tea, always ready to help anyone who called upon her.

After her separation from Jack, we stayed in touch when she lived in Nice, calling each other or meeting up from time to time. Nanou came almost every year to a gathering of former racers in Lyon, enjoying reuniting with her friends. The most loyal ones took her to Classic meetings where she met more ex-riders. She also attended the annual TT Riders meeting in the UK several times, where she was welcomed by all. We often called each other, and I took the opportunity to take notes on all the memories she liked to recall. In 2004, I published an interview with her in *Moto Légende* magazine. Like Jack's at the end of 1975, hers has its rightful place here. So let her tell her story ...

"I was born in 1928. My family's roots are in the Ain region, near Lyon. I was

Nanou feels stress while Jack leads the 1973 Senior TT.

two years old when my mother left my father, and I had to wait until I was around 12 or 13 years old to see her again. I got married at 17 to get myself free, and to be able to leave my family. I wanted to live a free and easy life, and it wasn't easy for a young girl at that time to do so. I got divorced six months later! I remarried a Frenchman, who took me to live in New York. Two years later, I returned to Paris, where I lived a bit of a bohemian existence, hanging out with artists. I posed as the Casque d'Or for a painter in Montmartre. One day, in a bistro, hearing English being spoken, I befriended a group. They were motorcycle racers, an activity I knew nothing about.

There was Reg Dearden, Dave Chadwick, Alan Trow, and two Frenchmen named Collot and Insermini. It was in 1956. I was first of all the girlfriend of Jacques Collot, then I moved in with Jacques Insermini. He was no ordinary man – he owned a garage, raced motorcycles, had done decathlon, triathlon, weights and dumbbells. He even ended his public career as a wrestler.

"I lived for almost seven years with Insermini. The nomadic and carefree life of motorcycle racers appealed to me. I met Jack Findlay in 1960: he had just crashed in a race at Clermont-Ferrand, and the circuit doctor

Left: Nanou with Daniele Fontana beside Jack on the grid of the 1970 Spanish GP in Barcelona.

Two pictures taken in the Spa paddock, in 1959 and 1969. Nanou was always elegant, even when cleaning a bike.

Nanou was always attentive to her rider and companion.

Nanou in 1960 beside Reg Dearden, Jacques Insermini's sponsor, and a youthful-looking Mike Hailwood.

was looking for an interpreter. That's how I became the paddock interpreter! But I wasn't particularly interested in Jack at the time. It was only later on that we ended up together. Insermini was thinking of retiring, but I had taken a liking to the Continental Circus. I couldn't see myself settling down again, so I stayed with Jack for over 15 years.

Left: Nanou was very careful about her appearance, even in bad weather like at the 1971 Ulster GP.
Top right: No electronic timing or TV screens back then, so the riders' wives and girlfriends had to be the timekeepers during practice and races.
Bottom right: A happy ending to the 1972 Formula 750 TT in which Jack finished third.

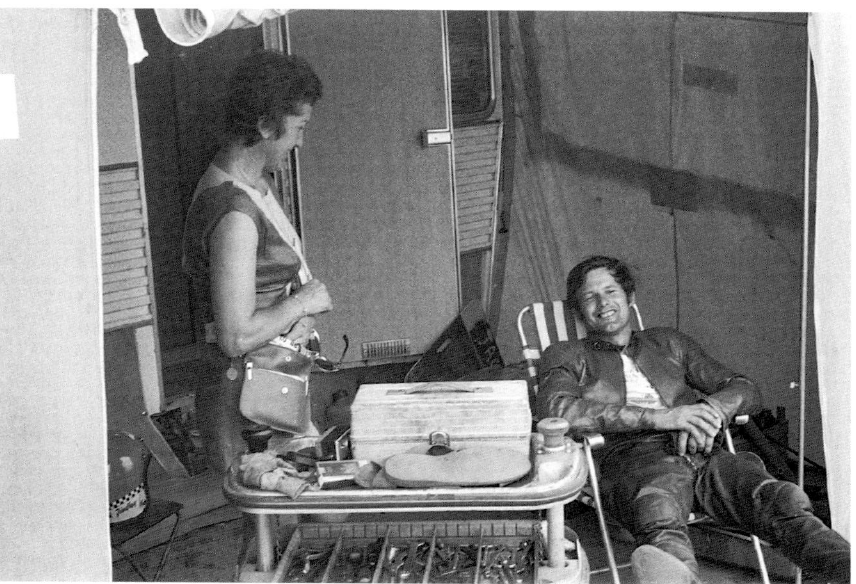

Top right: Nanou was a focal point in the paddock, always ready to help anyone.
Top left: A rider's wife or girlfriend had to cope with many different tasks.
Above: Life in the paddock was often carefree and happy.

"As regards money, I knew what Jack earned and spent. Everything went into racing, buying race bikes, trucks, maintenance, fuel. Fortunately, Jack quickly gained a good reputation. He was very well received in the small International races, where he was better paid than in the Grands Prix. Moreover, he didn't systematically seek out such events. If a race on the same day paid better, Jack would go there without hesitation. The organisers treated the riders so badly. I often fought to get something after a crash, for guys who were injured and didn't even have enough money to get home. What revolted me was that the toughest were always the organisers who had the most spectators, the most profits. Those guys were inflexible.

"The years went by, good and bad, depending on falls or breakdowns. From the mid-60s onwards, Jack experienced a certain level of comfort, finally enough to prepare for the following season properly. He was loved and respected by all, and then there was 1968, which was an extraordinary year. Jack was by far the best privateer in the world – he had already shown that in the previous two seasons. We were able to settle in Italy in the north of Milan, very close to Daniele Fontana's place, with whom Jack was very close. Our little apartment was always full; many friends came to see us. Jack had his workshop where he prepared and built his motorcycles in Fontana's factory. The 1968 season crowned three very good years, but then we experienced the hell described in the movie *Continental Circus*.

"When the offer came to ride for Linto in 1969, the coming year was supposed to be good. Jack had finally achieved the status of a works rider, so he no longer had to pay for and prepare his bikes himself. But right from the start it was a horror story, with breakdowns and crashes following one after the other. The Linto

British journalist Mick Woollett enjoyed a long friendship with Nanou and Jack.

MOTOR CYCLE WEEK ENDING 9 OCTOBER 1976

The girl who's been 'mum' and tea lady to riders all over Europe quits the circuits

We'll miss you, Nanou!

NANOU has handed out her last free cup of tea! Final race for the ...nch girl who has been a mother ...ure in the grand prix paddock for many years as most of us can ...ember, was the final Formula ...) round at Hockenheim.

"This is my twenty-first ...on. All of a sudden I feel ... tired. I still love the ...ng, especially the big ...s, but I don't enjoy life in ... paddock any more. It's ... to retire," said Nanou in ... matter-of-fact way.

...orn in Lyon she married ... the first time when she ... 17. It proved a mistake ... she was soon separated. ... first interest in motor ... it was car racing and it ... not until she was work... as an artist's model that ... came into contact with ...or cycles.

● NANOU pours a last cup of tea for MICK WOOLLETT who during his years as "Motor Cycle" Sports Editor rose high in the Nanou tea-drinker's league.

MICK WOOLLETT interviews a woman 2...

Artist

"One day I went to a ...urant with an artist. We ... into conversation with ... good-looking guys. They ... Jacques Collot and ...ues Insermini, two of ... leading French riders of ...e days."

...hat was in 1956. Nanou ... to a race at Moulins in ...ce with Insermini and they were married soon after. Ever since, she has been travelling Europe from circuit to circuit and she soon built up a reputation as mother-confessor, unofficial doctor, masseuse and provider of tea and snacks for all-comers.

"I must have served a million cups of tea. I remember that at Assen one year I was boiling the water in a gallon saucepan and serving 35 cups at a time!"

It was in her capacity as the paddock's leading first-aider that she met Jack Findlay, at Clermont-Ferrand in 1961. "He fell off during practising and did not want to go to hospital in case they tried to stop him racing."

Nanou treated him and a few months later they teamed up – and have been together ever since, travelling the circuits for seven months of the year and living in their flat in Milan during the winter.

What are the main changes in the racing scene during the last 21 seasons? "I think that in the old days, the Fifties, the riders were more friendly. They were a smaller, closer-knit group.

"I remember one race when the riders were on the grid and Bob Brown noticed that Jacques Insermini was not there. He held up the start and ran to the paddock to help Jacques who was changing a valve spring on

Mick Woollett wrote this article in Motor Cycle Weekly in October 1976, two years before Nanou's real retirement.

Jack and Nanou, the legendary couple in Continental Circus.

broke down so often that Jack had to borrow other motorcycles. When he crashed at Spa with Peter Williams' Matchless, we hit rock bottom. The bike was destroyed, and we had to pay for the damage. I admired Jack for his determination, because in those moments, he never looked back. In 1970 he started up again on his own. Then he built his 500 Jada with Daniele Fontana, finally won a Grand Prix, and obtained support from the Suzuki factory. Yet I had never heard him complain in all that awful time.

"These 20 years on the racing circuits have been intense for me, for I lived them without missing a moment. In the early 70s, my relationship with Jack deteriorated. The film *Continental Circus* had made us a celebrity couple, but in the paddock, the relationships of all the riders were put to the test. The riders were highly sought after, as were their wives and girlfriends! I loved this free and vagabond existence. I was in love with this indefinable thing that was the Continental Circus. I brushed off various advances – I respected Jack, but we never talked together about this passion that drove me on. Perhaps he noticed it, and yet it can't be said that I was more attached to the circus than to him. When the movie was released in 1972, our relationship was glorified publicly, even as we began to discuss separation.

"I don't like this film. The original project was to show a vice-world champion. The film was shot in the wrong year: Jack Findlay was more than just a rider who was always crashing. It should have been explained why he kept falling off, why the breakdowns kept accumulating. I was often told that I stole the spotlight from him, which is another reason why I don't like this movie. The racing was merciless, and so many riders died. We lived in an atmosphere of freedom, and fleeting pleasures.

Sometimes I had the feeling that Jack's dream would be to die on the track. I was so involved in his life that this idea was probably wrong. This man had extraordinary courage, but that courage led him into dangerous situations where he would need to express it even more. It was a kind of vicious circle. Jack was very discreet; he spoke little, even to me. He lived with his own secrets, but his love for motorcycles and his joy of racing were so strong. Jack was an idealist, meticulous, perfectionist, hence he was always dissatisfied with his own results.

Nanou with Jack and Roger Keen at the 1988 French GP at Paul Ricard.

"Separating from Jack was tough. I needed my freedom. I couldn't see myself with him outside the circuits. At the same time, a separation is always a difficult moment. I came back to live on the Côte d'Azur because I always loved that place, close to Insermini, with whom I remained friends.

"When my parents died, I was fortunate to inherit a small sum of money, which I invested while thinking of it as a kind of life insurance. I tightened my belt – there were tough moments, but I held on. Keeping these savings for myself wasn't a sign of

Nanou with her great friend Pat, Billie Nelson's widow, and Alberto Pagani at the Centennial TT in Assen in 1998.

Enjoying the sun in Nice in the early years of the new millennium.

Guided by Victoria Heenan, Nanou went to Mooroopna in 2006 for the unveiling of Jack's statue.

distrust in Jack, but a degree of prudence, because this life was so uncertain. And then I had a major health setback in 1981. I started losing my sight.

"Various operations and treatments failed, and I became blind in 1994. You live with this handicap because there's no other choice, but you never get used to it. So I decided to live as if everything was fine, going out with friends and visiting contacts from the Continental Circus, in Italy, England, and even Australia!"

Over the years, we called each other regularly. Jack and Nanou had met several times again, for she held immense affection for him. Without hesitation, she went to Australia in 2006 to attend the unveiling of Jack's bronze statue in his hometown of Mooroopna, as he couldn't make the trip due to his emphysema.

Jack's death two years later saddened her deeply; it was a definitive break from the world she had loved so much. I visited her regularly, in addition to our phone conversations. In her last years, her health declined, her eye disease progressed, causing suffering that she spoke of without ever complaining.

Nanou passed away in January 2023. Her funeral was attended mainly by friends from the Blind Association which had taken care of her, people who knew nothing of her past in motorcycle racing. But they all described the same cheerful, welcoming and generous woman who had charmed so many people in the paddocks of the Continental Circus.

To see or not to see

With Nanou, we had regular talks on the telephone, and I was taking notes of our conversations. She knew I was doing this, and was laughing about it.

Here are a few quotes from the time soon after she lost her sight.

"My visual memory is frozen since 1981. I joined a blind persons' association in 1982."

"It's very difficult to survive in the dark."

"When you live in the dark, the most depressing thing is that you never know if it is day or night."

"In the beginning, I was terrified anytime I had to go in the street. I was terribly afraid."

"Being blind is mainly a question of memory. You must remember where all the little things are that you need daily. If one day you don't put something back at the right place, you'll never find it again. When I walk in the streets, I count my footsteps, I check the pavement kerbs, I put my hand on the walls to find my way. What blind people fear the most is when their memory starts to fail."

One day, Nanou's illness became worse. She was living in a pitch-black world, but suddenly it became bright white. And it was very painful too.
"Living in the dark is awful, but the white is worse. It's been very difficult for me to accept it. At that time I really thought about jumping out of a window."

But Nanou always kept her optimism, and her joy for life. One day she said to me "Did you watch the football match? I cannot leave my television alone. I watch all the World Cup games. Yesterday it was really nice, I heard a good match."

She told me that she was also 'looking' at all the MotoGP races on TV, trying to imagine what was happening on the track.

During her final years, Nanou had a house carer. She also had a good friend living in the same building, Jamila, another blind person, who was cooking for her. Around her, many members of the Blind People's Association were helping, too.

One day, I took a tape recorder and recorded four tapes, reading one of my motorcycle books for her. I realised how hard it is to speak slowly and correctly – it takes time, and it is difficult. It made me understand how important it is that professional speakers or actors should record books for blind people. It's a generous and important thing for them to do.

Back in 2004, Nanou had to travel from Nice to Lyon, where she had an appointment with an eye specialist. She had to spend a night in a hotel before her visit the next morning to the hospital. It was complicated for her to find help outside her home city, so I jumped in a train and went to Lyon to take care of her during the evening. Somebody would come and pick her up the following morning and drive her to the doctor's appointment.

I booked a hotel room, so when she came to Lyon we went there. I explained to the hotel receptionist what was going on, and how they could help her, then I took her to her room. We went inside, and I was holding her hand. She asked me to 'drive' her while she 'visited' the room.

"Where are the walls? Help me touch the walls. This one has the door. Good. This one has a window?"

- Yes Nanou, here is the window.

"Good. Let's keep going. There's a little table against this wall, then on the other one a little cabinet to put my clothes in, is that right?"

- Yes, Nanou, exactly.

"Take me to the bathroom."

She touches everything, taking her time.

"Well, let's do another lap ... let's do it again, so I can memorise all that properly."

So we do it again, the walls, the window, the table, the bed, the bathroom.

"Perfect, now I know where I am. Let's go to the restaurant."

I was amazed. Nanou had done that dozens of times before when she used to travel to visit her old racing friends all over the world, mostly in England, but also in Italy and even Australia. She had to do that anytime she was arriving in an unknown place.

That day, I felt really fortunate to be in good health, which seems so natural to all of us who are. But for disabled people, everyday life is a daily fight.

Nanou walking with a friend in Nice in 2019.

CHAPTER 11

A New Life

1980-2000

When he decided to quit racing at the end of the 1978 season, Jack was going through a rough patch. For a few years, his relationship with Nanou had been on the rocks. Not only were they struggling to get along in their daily lives, but they also faced a kind of rejection in the paddock, where they were made to feel old. "The last two years have been tough," Nanou told me. "We were on the verge of separating at the end of the 1976 and 1977 seasons. But his two successive accidents in 1977 and 1978 meant I couldn't leave him just then – he really needed my help. When he decided to stop, our separation was inevitable, it was clear." Jack was well aware of this, because later he told journalist Mick Duckworth this terse sentence: "At the end of '78, I stopped racing and separated from Nanou. It wasn't the most glorious moment in my life."

The end of a career is always a difficult transition that worries all high-level athletes.

A typical shot from Jack's born-again existence as a Michelin tyre tester, riding a Honda CBX 1000 on the roads.

Two happy riders secretly testing Michelin's new radial tyres: Jean-Pierre Venessi and Jack.

Jack was accustomed to testing the early examples of Bimota's road bikes.

Jack riding a Bimota at the Misano race track.

On a visit to Michelin's Ladoux test centre, French President François Mitterrand met Jack and his fellow test riders.

Motorcycle racers were no exception because, except for a very few, they ended their careers without fortune or prospects. "By the end of 1978 I was washed up," Jack confessed. "Not just physically and mentally, but financially, too. I was broke. During the season, my truck with all my equipment inside was stolen in Italy. The thieves then contacted me to offer to return everything for a ransom, which I paid, but between that incident and my health problems from my crashes, it was really a nightmare season. It was time for all of that to stop. I was broke. I had nothing left."

While Nanou decided to settle in La Ciotat after selling all her equipment, Jack made trips back and forth to Italy, where he kept contacts. The Bimota company asked him to carry out tests for its new range of chassis designed to accommodate Suzuki engines. In 1978, Bimota decided to launch a range of big-engined road bikes, the first of which was the SB2 using a GSX-R 1000 engine. Jack took part in the tests and their presentation at trade shows. Bimota had an agreement with Michelin, which was starting to develop a radial motorcycle tyre. This work took place at the Research Center in Ladoux, near Clermont-Ferrand, which had workshops and various test tracks, including a banked speed oval.

Jack and Jean-Pierre reading a very technical document.

"In 1979, I joined the team of testers that Michelin had just set up to develop new tyres for large-capacity road bikes," said former test rider Jean-Pierre Venessi. "The following year, we saw Jack Findlay arrive at Ladoux accompanied by our engineer François Decima, who announced that he was going to join our group. We were very impressed to see him arrive, but his kindness and modesty quickly made us forget his glorious track record."

Jack established a base in Clermont-Ferrand and began a new life: testing high-performance tyres, both those intended for new road models and those developed for

Jack testing the first SB2 Bimota at the Mugello circuit.

A technical stop during a test session in the south of France.

competition machines. "From that moment on, I rode the fastest motorcycles in the world on the test tracks and on the roads," he said. "There was a team of outstanding technicians to prepare all these machines. One of my favourite bikes was an 1100 Bimota Suzuki, whose engine was prepared by Jean-Pierre Fehr. On the speed oval at Ladoux I was clocked on it at 300km/h. At the time, with such a heavy bike, it was extraordinary."

Jack tirelessly conducted tests on Michelin tracks and long road tests, which took him to all corners of Europe. The products developed with Bimota were the M48 and A48 with five layers of banding. Then he also played a decisive role in the development of the new radial competition tyre which Michelin introduced in 1985. His natural discretion was an asset for the manufacturer, because the secret of this revolution on two wheels had been well kept.

Jack with Doctor Claudio Costa, who twice saved his life when he crashed in Imola at the end of his racing career.

"Our team consisted of four testers, including Jack, who joined us for periods of eight or ten days at a time," recounts Jean-Pierre Venessi. "He also did tests for Bimota in Italy. We rode on public roads and race tracks. I remember testing at the Nürburgring, where Jack showed us around the track for three laps, before disappearing off into the distance after just a handful of turns! In winter, we went riding near Fréjus, where Michelin had a test base for cars and trucks. We rode on the A road between Le Muy and Mandelieu, or on the newly opened Autoroute. Luckily, we had some police friends to help us in case of any speeding checks. I remember Jack at the Mandelieu police station, saying with his lovely accent, 'Me Australian, me no understand,' and laughing out loud when the policeman let him go. And then, in 1987, he had that accident in Jerez: a car he

Jack with the Dorna team who worked at each Grand Prix. Paul Butler is fourth from right.

Left, top to bottom:
Jack was MotoGP technical supervisor for more than a decade.
Jack and Dominique spent 25 years together studiously avoiding any form of publicity.
Jack with Philippe Monneret, then a TV commentator for Eurosport's Grand Prix coverage.

was overtaking turned left in front of him. Jack got up, limping badly, but when they opened the leg of his riding suit, they saw that his knee was badly injured. This guy seemed insensitive to pain." This period testing bikes came to an end after this accident in southern Spain, when a cranial trauma was detected.

Over the next four years, Jack kept a low profile. He moved to Vaucresson, near Paris, living with Dominique Monneret, the ex-wife of Georges Monneret, the great French champion who'd passed away in 1984. Dominique had a fashion boutique in Versailles, and Jack helped her with various daily tasks. "I'm a courier, I drive a van, and I play tennis," he once told me, laughing, during a brief encounter, without giving further details. In fact, he had discovered a real passion for tennis, training like a fanatic, and was quickly complimented by top-ranked players who played him. "At first, I struggled because of my various leg injuries, but I progressed so quickly and loved the sport so much that I regretted not discovering it earlier, when I was young. I could have become a professional, and it would have been less risky than those damn motorcycles!"

Jack and Dominique always sought a certain discretion regarding the motorcycle racing scene. Only a few close friends learned that they had got married in the early 1990s, at a time when he was once again sought after to put his skills to use.

Jack is pictured with his faithful McIntyre Matchless during a Classic meeting in Montlhéry in 2001.

Dominique and Jack together during the 1992 Brazilian Grand Prix.

In early 1992, he was contacted by Paul Butler. This former Dunlop Racing Service manager had later worked at Yamaha, before helping American world champion Kenny Roberts create his 500cc Grand Prix team. In the late 1980s, Butler joined IRTA, the Grand Prix Teams' Association. "I met Jack in 1969 when I became head of Dunlop's competition service. I immediately hit it off with him as well as with Nanou, who was completely symbolic of those women willing to do anything to help their rider. I have a memory of that 1969 season linked to the Linto, such a fragile bike. It was better to put warm oil in the engine before starting it, and without hesitation, like other such women, Nanou would heat that oil on the little stove in their caravan."

For the 1992 season, IRTA was looking for a new technical supervisor. "I immediately suggested Jack," Butler said, "because he was respected by everyone, and

STATUE UNVEILING

Champ honoured

It was a day for memories, mates, and motorcycles.

On Saturday, several hundred motorcyclists descended on a strip of grass in a small country town to honour an unsung two-wheeled hero.

Jack Findlay was born in 1935 opposite the site in Mooroopna where his statue was unveiled before a crowd of family members, fans and enthusiasts who had travelled from far and wide for the occasion.

Representatives of Motorcycling Australia, the Federation of International Motorcyclists, the motorsport industry, and local and state politicians watched as Jack's brother and sister Rob and Jo unveiled a life-sized $25 000 bronze statue by Elphinstone artist Phil Mune depicting the world champion rider aboard his favourite Suzuki.

Earlier, more than 300 motorcycles gathered at Victoria Park Lake in Shepparton before riding in convoy with police escort over the Peter Ross-Edwards Causeway for the unveiling.

Jack Findlay, who was born in Northgate St directly opposite the statue site, left for England in 1958 to pursue a motorcycle racing career.

After 15 years as a privateer, battling the big money of factory teams, he won the Isle of Man TT and in 1975 he beat racing legend Barry Sheene to take the FIM 750cc World Championship title.

His achievements could have gone unrecognised in his hometown if it wasn't for the efforts of a small band of loyal admirers including Trevor Huggard, Noel Heenan, Mick Pettifer, Robert McLean and Kevin Simmonds who badgered local councillors, politicians, motorsport industry figures and local businesses to raise the money for the life-sized statue of their hero.

Saturday's ceremony was the culmination of eight years of hard work by Findlay's fans.

"This is a magnificent day, and it just shows what country people can do when they set their minds to it," Mr Heenan said.

Jack Findlay is now 71 and lives in Paris.

Rob Findlay, who lives in Melbourne, said his brother was suffering from the effects of emphysema after years of breathi racing fuel fumes and was now unable to travel.

"He would love to be here — No and the boys have done a magnificent job," Rob said.

He remembered Jack as a daredevil with a steely determination to win.

"I remember when he was a teenager he climbed the Mooroop water tower and hung by his boots from the top — he was always determined and wild," Rob said.

Saturday ended with a presentation dinner attended by more than 200 people at Mooroopna's Sir Ian McLennan Centre.

Jack Findlay's brother Rob and his sister Joan after unveiling the lif size statue in Mooroopna.

In 2006, the city of Mooroopna recognised its famous champion.

he had a great knowledge of racing. He immediately set up a system to record and control all incidents occurring during a Grand Prix meeting, even the most trivial ones. He then used this data to improve safety and to evolve the regulations. He was particularly vigilant about problems related to the fuels used. Over a ten-year period, his effectiveness improved a lot of things."

Again, Jack's discretion was not the least of his assets. Unless you went to find him in the room where he inspected the bikes and carried out all his checks, there was little chance of seeing him in the paddock. His pride was then to see his Australian compatriot Mick Doohan dominate the 500 GP category.

At the same time as his return to the race tracks, this time as a technician, Jack met his son Greg, whose existence he had never revealed, even though the secret had finally been leaked by Nanou at the time of their separation. Nanou had also told me one day, "Jack never talks about his son, but he thinks about him, and I often told him he shouldn't hesitate to try to meet him."

The Jack Findlay Memorial in Mooroopna.

But finally, the meeting took place in the early 1990s, as Greg himself wrote to me: "One of my New Zealand friends tracked down Jack and his wife Dominique in Paris, following an article he had read in a motorcycle magazine, while we were in Frankfurt, Germany, on a business trip together. We drove to Paris to meet up with Jack and Dominique. This meeting was wonderful for both of us, a prelude to many blissful years where we reunited for vacations in New Zealand, Australia, Thailand, or France, playing tennis, and jogging on the trails above Mandelieu. I am particularly happy that he was able to meet my two eldest daughters, Chloé and Sophie, who still talk about their Popa Jack, remembering the good times we spent together. I was also with Jack during his last moments. After his funeral, we scattered his ashes in the south of France. I was also at Le Mans for the commemorative race held in his honour."

Jack and Dominique often enjoyed the sun and the sea in Mandelieu, where Dominique had an apartment. She was not interested in motorcycles, and did not want to accompany Jack when he went to Classic motorcycle meetings, which had begun to flourish all over Europe in the 1990s. So Jack went alone to the Centennial TT in Assen in 1998, where he took the handlebars of his McIntyre Matchless. That year, very discreetly, he attended the Coupes Moto Légende at the Montlhéry circuit, before returning more officially three years later and posing for posterity with the McIntyre G50 taken there by Mick Hemmings, the British enthusiast who had restored it, and now raced it in Classic events such as the Goodwood Revival. But Jack rarely attended these commemorations, because he did not like to dwell on the past, he often said. It was also because he did not want to revive memories of the Continental Circus that bound him inseparably to Nanou, while he shared his life with Dominique. This did not prevent him from maintaining good relations with Nanou and with his old friend Jacques Insermini. They often called each other and also saw each other from time to time, their old friendship still uniting them.

Jack directed the Technical Service of the Grand Prix series until 2002. On the evening of the last Grand Prix of the season, on 21 September, in Rio de Janeiro, he was taken unwell in his hotel room, where he remained unconscious for nearly 24 hours. Returning to France, he underwent a series of medical examinations, which determined abnormalities in the circulation of the cerebrospinal fluid that surrounds and protects the brain and spinal cord. This was a consequence of all his several falls, and especially the terrible head traumas suffered after his last major

Jack's victorious 750 Yamaha was on display when the statue to him was unveiled in Mooroopna.

accidents in '77 and '78. Since flying was not recommended for him anymore, he left his position as Grand Prix technical supervisor for a well-deserved retirement.

"Jack and my mother greatly enjoyed the years they spent together," says Philippe Monneret, Dominique's son. "My mother sometimes accompanied him to a Grand Prix in a distant country, but she wasn't interested in motorcycles. She would have liked to go on cruises with Jack, but he absolutely refused. He said he hated boat trips since his journeys between Australia and England at the very beginning of his career. I always got along really well with Jack – he was very funny, and always cheerful. But the last few years were difficult. He and my mother were always in Mandelieu, for Jack loved that place. In the end, Dominique is the woman he lived with the longest."

Gradually after the Rio incident, Jack suffered from repeated discomfort. He then suffered from severe respiratory failure, which affected his final year of life. Short of breath, he could no longer move, so had to lie down with oxygen assistance, and had difficulty holding a conversation. We spoke several times during his last months. He retained his sharp mind and underlying humour, but the cheerful tone of the past had disappeared. Uttering just a few words exhausted him horribly. "I look at the sea," he replied when I asked him what he spent his days doing. With Dominique by his side, he passed away in their apartment in Mandelieu on Saturday, 19 May, 2007. By a pure coincidence, that same day, his compatriot Anthony West qualified for the French MotoGP race, which was to take place the following day.

Jack Findlay's results (1958/1978)

24 podiums in World Championship races including

3 GP 500 cc wins :
Ulster 1971, Tourist Trophy 1973, Austria 1977
24 international successes, 40 podiums
4 victories in Formula 750 racing

Positions in the World Championship: (category/rank)

1961: 500/16
1963: 500/8 - 250/18
1964: 500/14
1965: 500/7
1966: 500/3 - 250/7 - 50/17
1967: 500/5 - 250/14
1968: 500/2 - 350/18
1969: 500/13 - 350/6 - 250/36
1970: 500/7 - 350/21
1971: 500/5 - 350/35
1972: 500/8 - 350/10
1973 - 500/5
1974: 500/5
1975: 500/10 - 750/1
1976: 500/8 - 350/33 - 750/13
1977: 500/16 - 750/4

Racing bikes ridden by Jack Findlay during his career

Part of the game was that all Continental Circus riders raced in many different classes with a surprising number of bikes and engines. The bikes that Jack raced were:

50 class: Bridgestone (twin)
125 class: Montesa, Bultaco, Maico (single), Honda (twin)
250 class: Mondial, Cotton, Aermacchi (single), DMW, Yamaha (twin)
350 class: AJS, Norton, Aermacchi (single), Jawa (4-cyl), Yamaha (twin)
500 class: Norton, Matchless, Aermacchi (single), Cardani (3-cyl), Linto, Jada, Suzuki (twin), König, Suzuki, Yamaha (4-cyl)
750 class: Moto-Guzzi, Norton (twin), Suzuki (3-cyl), Yamaha (4-cyl)
1000 cc endurance: Honda (4-cyl)
Land Records : 500 Norton mono - 500 BMW twin

Acknowledgements

I would like to say thank you to all the following people and organisations.

Leo Darveniza who contacted me in October 2023 asking for documentation about Jack Findlay. With his friend Noel Heenan, they have restored the 750 Yamaha on which Jack won the 1975 F750 Championship. One message after another, they asked me to write this book and I want to thank them for this idea.

All my sources, that I contacted after checking what I had in my own archives, first of all Don Cox in Australia, where his books about Australian racers are a world reference. Don reminded me that we met long time ago in Daytona Beach, Florida, and immediately gave me all informations he had about Findlay's early years in Australia.

The following long-time friends, collecting and keeping archives about motorcycle racing: François-Marie Dumas and Didier Ganneau in France, Philip Tooth in England, Dieter Mutschler in Germany, who once again gave me full help. I can never thank them enough.

Other friends: photographers, Frenchmen François Beau and Christian Lacombe, Dutchman Jan Burgers who did the same, giving spontaneous help, and this applies to all the other names in the credit list. Special thank you for Jérôme Lapperrousaz, always keen to speak about his friendship with Jack and provide pictures of his movie *Continental Circus*.

Websites RacingMemo.free.fr created by the late Vincent Glon (unfortunately killed in a road accident on his motorcycle), and Sidonie Thouvenin's pilotegpmoto.com, as both are precious sources. Thank you also to Didier Fort who gave me his results compilations, which were so helpful to follow Findlay's career race after race.

Finally, I have to give a special thank you to Dominique Findlay and her son Philippe Monneret, who opened Jack's personal archives for me, which they have carefully kept. Among them were many pictures, most of them from unknown fans.

I also want to mention specially my old friend Jarda Sejk, who gave me many pictures a long time ago. I want to honour his memory and his kindness because Jarda was living in Czechoslovakia. He produced reports under very difficult conditions, as going to Western Europe was not easy for him as a citizen of the ex-Soviet bloc, and using a simple, old-fashioned camera. But he had such enthusiasm and passion for motorcycle racing that I never forgot him.

Jacques Bussillet

Photo credits

Archives Findlay/Monneret: 9, 10, 11, 12, 39 (middle), 41 (bottom), 45, 53, 93 (bottom), 151, 152, 153 (bottom); including Jarda Sejk 43, 55 (bottom), 56 (top), 59 (bottom), 61, 74 (top), Kirkpatrick 44 , Wolfgang Gruber 60 (left), 62 (top) and Bernagozzi 64

Archives Andrée Lyonnard/Nanou 143

Don Cox and bikesandbathurst.com.au: 11, 20 (top), 21

Union Motocycliste de l'Ain: 11, 20 (bottom), 27 (top) 33, 40 (top), 75 (bottom)

La Vie de la Moto Archives: 25, 26, 31 (bottom), 47

Dieter Mutschler Archives: 37 (bottom), 38 , 51, including

Mick Woollett: 51 (top), 55 (top), 70 (top), 76 (top), 77 (bottom) , and Karl Schleuter 40 (centre), 50(top)

Tooth-Greening Archives: 15, 41 (top), 42, 48, 51 (bottom), 56, 59 (top), 62 (bottom), 71 (bottom), 98, 100, 101 -103 (top)

Henri Lallemand: 17, 19, 22, 23 (bottom), 24, 28 (bottom), 29, 31 (top), 34, 35, 65, 138 (bottom right), 139 (top right)

La Montagne daily in Clermont-Ferrand: 23 (top)

Carlo Perelli: 58 (top right)), 65 (bottom)

Christian Lacombe: 49, 56 (bottom), 59 (bottom), 60 (right), 61, 79, 82, 83, 103 (bottom)

Didier Ganneau: 53

Maurice Bula: 75

François Beau: 52, 67, 69, 70 (bottom), 71 (top), 72 (top), 75 (bottom), 76, 78, 84, 85 (bottom), 91(top), 92 (top), 93 (top), 99 (bottom), 101 (bottom), 102 (bottom), 104, 106, 107, 108, 110, 111, 112, 113 (bottom) , 116, 117, 118, 119, 120, 121, 125 (bottom), 126 , 127, 132 (top), 133 (top), 135 (bottom)

Jean-Pierre Venessi: 147, 148, 149 (bottom), 150

Jérôme Laperrousaz/ Film *Continental Circus*: 72 (centre), 73, 74 (bottom), 95 (bottom), 96, 97, 138 (bottom left)

Jean-Pierre Boulmé: 128 (centre & bottom)

Jan Burgers: 90 (top), 129 (top) 134 (top left)

JP Edart: 100 (bottom left), 137

Jacques Chaudy: 15, 30

Jean Castanier: 124

Damien Follenfant: 68

Christian Bouchet: 139 (colour), 142

Pierre Gabriele: 134

Leo Darveniza /Noel Heenan: 144, 155, 156

Daytona Speedway/Dave Friedman: 99 (top)

Bimota/*Motosprint*: 148 (right)

Michelin: 149 (top)

Jean-Pierre Pradères: 153 (top)

Jacques Bussillet: 12 (bottom) 13, 57, 58 (top left), 64 (top), 65 (top), 81, 85 (top), 86, 87, 88, 89, 90, 91 (centre & bottom), 95 (top), 105, 113 (top), 115, 122, 125 (top) -127 (bottom), 128 (top), 130, 131, 132 (centre & bottom), 133 (bottom), 135 (top), 138 (bottom left), 139 (top left and down), 140, 141, 146

Index

Featured circuits: